The Secret History of Human Resets

THE GREAT MUD FLOOD OF 1834, THE 1587 PLASMA EVENT, THE BIBLICAL FLOOD, AND OTHER HISTORICAL RESET THEORIES

Donny Davis

Preface:

For years, a group of conspiracy theorists have been investigating the possibility that a catastrophic mud flood swept across the world in the mid-19th century, wiping out entire civilizations and burying cities under layers of mud and debris. They believe humans have gone through multiple resets such as this throughout time. While the theory is controversial and has been met with skepticism by mainstream scholars, a growing number of people have become convinced that there is something to the mud flood hypothesis.

This book is an exploration of the mud flood theory and its implications. Through extensive research and analysis of historical records, eyewitness accounts, and scientific evidence, we will examine the possibility that a global cataclysmic event occurred in the 19th century, reshaping the world as we know it today. From the mysterious architecture of buildings allegedly built before the mud flood to the anomalous artifacts and artifacts that suggest a lost advanced civilization, we will delve into the mysteries surrounding this controversial theory.

Introduction

The internet is abuzz with conspiracy, mystery, and crazy theories to explain the past, present, and future. Concerns about fake news have morphed into concerns about fake history. Obsessions with secret societies controlling the present transform into obsessions that they cooked the past. Perhaps the deep state must divulge surprising truths, yet combine them with total fakery so mainstream people simply push it all away!

This book documents the latest greatest theory: The Mud Flood Reset. Along with all of its tag-along theories: Tartaria, Flat Earth, Giants, Cyclical Time. Put on your seat belt, and be prepared to have your worldview turned upside down.

The Mud Flood
What is the Mud Flood Theory? What is the Evidence?

What if the history you are taught in textbooks is a lie? What if real history has been hidden from us?

The Mud Flood theory proposes that humanity had an advanced civilization as little as 200 years ago. It suffered a catastrophic flood worldwide in the 1800s which covered cities with a layer of mud between 6-12 feet deep. Afterwards, there was a systematic cover-up that this event occurred, and our civilization was reset to a more primitive culture with forgotten knowledge.

Evidence of a worldwide mud flood might be found in old historic buildings in which windows or doors are below ground level. Or in old photographs showing streets caked in mud.

Adherents of the mud flood theory believe this mud flood was accompanied by a depopulation event. Historic photographs seem to show fully built, but empty cities. Perhaps a previous civilization built our cities, then suffered a cataclysm in which a large percentage of people perished.

The elite may have systematically covered up this mud flood and encouraged people to repopulate the earth in the 1880s. People who were "in on it" taught the new population a false historical narrative in orphanages, boarding schools, and workhouses for children.

Subscribers to this theory also believe that people in the 18th century had ancient technology that was more advanced than we have today, and that this technology was lost during the reset. Ancient technology may have included antique fireplaces that heated and cooled houses, airships for travel, and steam-powered machines which hooked into ancient steam tunnels. Ancient civilizations may have built most of the infrastructure we enjoy today with advanced technology. Today's modern people may have inherited this infrastructure which required only minimal work to repair and modernize.

Perhaps genetic resets accompany historic resets. People may have been more intelligent and lived longer. People could have been taller in the past before experiencing a reset. This may explain why older buildings seem much larger in scale.

We could be a replacement civilization of the previous one. We may have inherited all the wonders of the previous civilization without being told anything about it. Perhaps ancient architectural structures were created with advanced unknown technologies, but we are told these structures were built with hand tools and hard work. Maybe we are not a progressive society with more technology than in the past. Human history could consist of a series of cycles, separated by resets. These resets could involve disasters such as fires, floods,pandemics, and nuclear war. This book will examine all of these theories in detail. We could be a species with amnesia. In essence, humanity rises from the ashes like a Phoenix.

Amazing Architecture Built With Hand Tools?

Were Old Architectural Structures Built With Primitive Tools, or With Ancient Technology?

Did ancient people really build the wonders of the world without advanced technology? Did they really build all the fantastic architectural structures we enjoy today with primitive hand tools?

We are told that ancient people had no power drills, electric cranes, automatic manufacturing, or electric motors. The first steam shovel was invented in 1839. The first electric crane did not appear until 1876. The first power drill was designed in 1895 and required multiple operators. The first gasoline powered tractor was built in 1892.

But how did our ancestors build some of the structures we see today? Historians struggle to explain how ancient people built the amazing structures throughout history without high tech tools. Perhaps we do not live in a progressive society, and ancient people had more knowledge than we do today.

1

Monolithic Stone Structures

We are told that people who lived in the past did not have access to the advanced tools, machinery, and technology that are available today. Mainstream experts say our ancestors had to rely on their hands, basic tools, and the natural resources around them to accomplish tasks such as quarrying limestone rocks and assembling them into structures.

Yet, our ancestors managed to build monolithic stone structures such as the Egyptian and Aztec pyramids or the Moai statues of Easter Island. The pyramids are remarkable works of architecture. These massive stone structures, with their precise dimensions and complex internal passages, are a feat of engineering that still inspires awe and admiration today. The sheer scale of the pyramids is staggering. The Great Pyramid of Giza, for example, stands 481 feet tall and is composed of 2.3 million stone blocks, some weighing up to 80 tons. The general theory is that the huge stones, weighing 2.5 tons-80 tons each, were carved from the quarries using copper chisels and wooden mallets. Then, these blocks were dragged using rollers, sledges, and barges. Workers lifted stones into position using ramps, cranes, and pulleys. However, such work cannot be replicated today using these rudimentary methods. Perhaps our ancestors possessed ancient technology to accomplish such engineering feats, but this knowledge was lost in a human reset.

Giza Pyramids[2]

Moai at Rano Raraku, Easter Island

Great Sphinx of Giza[28]

Megalithic Stone Structures

Ancient people built megalithic stone structures with multiple large stones globally between the 4th 15th Centuries. These stones often weighed 100 tons or more. These stones fit together like a jigsaw puzzle with such precision that a credit card cannot be inserted in the mortarless joints. This style of architecture is found not just in Peru at Sacsayhuaman, but all over the world. Allegedly, builders quarried enormous stones weighing up to 200 tons each, cut them to precision, and lifted them into place without the use of power saws, hydraulic cranes, or machines. These stone structures were highly resistant to natural disasters such as earthquakes or floods. People built these structures in the exact same way on different continents before there was any means of global travel or communication. Most of these structures were systematically taken apart and destroyed so that the stones could be reused in new buildings. The remains we see today are only a small portion of the structures that once stood in ancient times. Were these structures merely built with primitive hand tools, or with ancient technology? Did ancient people have unknown techniques like melting and pouring geopolymers into molds? Why can't we explain how these stone structures were built?

The stone wall of Nijo-jo, Japan, completed in 1603[3]

Sacsayhuaman in Cuzco, Peru[4]

The Lion Gate at Mycenae, Greece, built 1250 BC[5]

Stepwells of the East

Other amazing structures that were built before any modern tools include the stepwells of the east. We are told these structures were hand carved from stone. Yet they contain identical patterns and precise geometry consistent throughout the structure. These structures seem too perfect to have been built by hand.

Adalaj stepwell from above carved in sandstone, built 1499[7]

Sun temple Surya kund Stepwell adjoining the temple, built 1026-27 AD[8]

Rani ki vav is an intricately constructed stepwell situated in the town of Patan in Gujarat, India[9]

Chad Baori stepwell[10]

Hindu Temples

Structures like the Lakshmi Narasimha temple and Kailasha Mandir, Ellora are not built anymore. The entire Mandir above, like many Hoysala temples, was cut out from solid basalt bedrock, from top to bottom. Nearly 400,000 tons of stone was dug to create this marvel. Surprisingly no debris is found up to 100 kms radius of the Mandir.

Some Hindu Practitioners say these structures were not made with chisels and hammers. But were created with advanced Ancient Bharatiya Technology. Many believe that this knowledge was lost in the burning of Nalanda University.

11

Le temple de Brihadishwara (Tanjore, India)

Lakshmi Narasimha temple

Kailash Temple

Star Forts

Star forts are what mainstream historians call Bastion Forts. These were built in the late 15th and early 16th centuries, all over the world. These forts were designed during an era of gunpowder and the cannon, we are told. The geometric design of the nation's military allegedly protected against blind spots during conflict. Our ancestors supposedly did not have the technology to view structures from above, but somehow were able to build this precise geometric patterning for protection from war. How did they manage to achieve this without advanced technology?

Fort Bourtange, Netherlands

Fort Manjarabad, Karnataka, India

Fuerte de Nuestra Señora de Gracia, Elvas, Portugal [14]

Cathedrals

Cathedrals were also built before any modern power tools, according to mainstream historians. Experts tell us cathedrals were built by skilled tradesmen using hand tools such as pickaxes, hammers, braces, chisels, and saws. Builders also used ancient cranes with ropes and pulleys. However, the level of skill, precision, and geometry evident in the work makes it seem impossible to have been accomplished with primitive tools. This level of craftsmanship is not generally replicated today. They don't build them like this anymore!

Duomo di Milano in Milan[17]

18

Notre Dame in Paris.

Canals

Another great feat of architecture of our 'primitive' ancestors were canals. One great example is the Erie Canal in America. The Erie Canal was allegedly built between 1817 and 1825. The canal spans 363 miles and was 12 meters wide and four meters deep. Mainstream historians claim Irish immigrants used shovels, axes, black powder, and oxes to clear the land, and cut through 80 feet of hard limestone known as the Niagra Escarpment. They built this canal with complicated aqueducts and locks in a span of seven years.

Lockport - showing the Erie Canal's complicated series of locks.

The Erie Canal once crossed the Genesee River by an aqueduct in Rochester. The above picture does not show a bridge with a car on top, but a canal with a boat traversing a river! This aqueduct was first built in 1825, and replaced in 1842. It became the center of the two-mile underground portion of the Rochester Subway in 1927 and operated until 1956. The tunnel remains under Broad Street and continues to spark the imagination of Rochester residents and city planners. All built without modern tools.

Global Societies of the Past

People from the past may have had the means to travel globally. Mainstream historians have suggested that ancient people were not capable of global travel or communication, but evidence suggests otherwise. Similar structures can be found all over the world, indicating a global cohesiveness over time.

Pyramids

Not only are structures such as pyramids constructed globally at the same time, but it appears that global structures also fade away in synchronization across the globe, as if all regions undergo a reset simultaneously. Despite the fact that the disappearance of certain building styles, like the megalithic stone structures in Peru, is frequently attributed to the collapse of local empires, we often disregard the similarity in how these architectural structures vanish simultaneously worldwide. The possibility of global resets is ignored, even though we no longer construct buildings in the same manner and lack knowledge of their original construction methods.

19

Asia

South America

Europe (Not Excavated Yet) [23]

31

Sphinx Structures Around the World

Sphinx Structures are found all over the world. Sphinxes are mythological creatures with the body of a lion and the head of a human or other animal.

In ancient Egyptian mythology, the sphinx was often depicted with the head of a pharaoh, and was considered a symbol of royal power and authority. The Sphinx was believed to be a guardian of sacred places, serving as a protector of the pharaohs and the afterlife. The Sphinx was often placed at the entrance of temples and tombs to ward off evil spirits and protect the sacred space from intruders. The most famous example of an Egyptian sphinx is the Great Sphinx of Giza, which has the head of a pharaoh and is believed to date back to the 4th dynasty of the Old Kingdom.

In Greek mythology, the sphinx was often depicted as a female creature with the head of a human, the body of a lion, and the wings of a bird. In this context, the sphinx was often associated with riddles and puzzles, and was said to pose a riddle to travelers that they had to solve in order to pass. The most famous of these riddles was "What walks on four legs in the morning, two legs in the afternoon, and three legs in the evening?" The answer was a human, who crawls on all fours as a baby, walks on two legs as an adult, and uses a cane in old age. The Sphinx's purpose in Greek mythology was to test the intelligence of humans and serve as a symbol of wisdom.

Many associate the sphinx with the Astrological Sign or Age of Leo. Pictured on this page are sphinx statues from Russia [23], Romania[24], Crimea [25], Argentina [26], Pakistan [27], and Egypt [28].

Russia

Romania

Crimea

Argentina

Egypt

Pakistan

33

The Parthenon And Structures With Columns

Structures similar to the Parthenon in Athens, Greece include buildings in Athens, Greece [29], Italy [30], St. Petersburg, Russia from the Crimean Civil War [31], Lebanon [32], Germany [33], and Tennessee, USA.[34] The Parthenon is an iconic temple located in Athens, Greece, and was built in the 5th century BCE. It is widely considered to be one of the greatest examples of classical Greek architecture and is an important symbol of ancient Greek civilization. Columns, particularly the classical Greek Doric, Ionic, and Corinthian columns, have become an iconic symbol of Western architecture. The columns themselves are symbolic of strength, stability, and order, and are often used to convey a sense of grandeur and importance. Columns are also an important architectural feature that serve a functional purpose in supporting the weight of buildings and distributing that weight evenly to the ground.

Athens, Greece   Italy   Crimean Civil War

Lebanon   Germany   Tennessee, USA

Arches around the Globe

Arches built with a similar style are found all over the globe. The arches shown below are from Munich[35], Afghanistan [36], Libya[37], Brooklyn, New York[38], and Washington Square Park, NY[39]. Arches often have many architectural features, such as windows. These openings are located within arches that may be designed to align with the sun on celestial events such as equinoxes or solstices. Arches have an elegant and graceful appearance, with a smooth curve that can create a sense of movement and flow. They are impressive engineering feats, as they are able to support a great deal of weight without collapsing. Arches with a neoclassical style were generally built during the 18th and 19th centuries, particularly in the period between the 1760s and the 1830s. They fell out of favor during the late 19th and early 20th centuries, possibly due to a reset.

Munich

Afghanistan

Libya

Brooklyn, New York

Washington Square Park, New York

Domes around the World

Structures with domes are found all over the world. Many believe they represent the pregnant stomach of the Mother Goddess. Domes are inherently strong and stable structures, thanks to their curved shape. The curved shape of domes also makes them excellent for enhancing sound. In large spaces such as cathedrals or concert halls, domes can help amplify sound and ensure that it is evenly distributed throughout the space. Domes are often admired for their beauty, particularly when they are embellished with intricate designs or mosaics. They can create a sense of grandeur and awe, particularly in religious buildings. Domes have played an important role in many cultures and religions throughout history. For example, the dome of the rock in Jerusalem is an iconic symbol of Islam, while the dome of St. Peter's Basilica in Rome is a symbol of the Catholic Church. Most of these domes, especially with metal roofs, were built in the 18th and 19th Century.

Obelisks Around the World

Obelisks are found all over the world including in Sydney[40] , Istanbul [41] , Ethiopia [42] , Munich [43] , Rome[44 ,] and Israel [45] . They are tall, slender structures that rise up to a pointed tip, representing a phallus or a ray of sunlight. They have been associated with concepts such as power, strength, and stability, and were often used as symbols of religious or political significance. They are engineering marvels, as they are made from a single piece of stone, which had to be quarried, transported, and erected with great precision. Obelisks were often erected to mark important places, such as temples, tombs, or public spaces. The most famous obelisks were built during the ancient Egyptian period, specifically during the New Kingdom period between 1550 BC and 1070.

Istanbol   Sydney   Ethiopia

Rome   Munich   Israel

BC._____

Empty Muddy Cities of the 19th Century

Why do cities in the 19th Century seem so empty and muddy? Did humanity suffer a worldwide depopulation event?

Historical photographs of different cities may indicate that the world suffered a depopulation event. Cities in historical aerial photographs seem like they are built for hundreds of thousands of people, yet appear empty and muddy.

St. Petersburg, 1860

This is St. Petersburg. The population of St. Petersburg was allegedly 500,000 people in 1860. And yet, nobody is visible in the photographs. Where is everyone? Why are the cities so vast if the population was only 500,000 in each? This ghost city looks like it could hold millions of people.

St. Isaac's Cathedral.

Why is this city so built out if it has such few people? Did city designers plan for population growth in advance?

Mainstream historians might say the photographer took these picture before people woke up, and therefore the city seems empty. It is likely morning time since Alexander Column casts a long shadow. Long shadows only occur during morning or evening. If this picture was taken around 10 in the morning, wouldn't there be more people up and about on the streets?

These buildings seem expensive, well built, and beautiful. Yet the streets look dumpy and torn up. Did ancient people not have a way to pave the streets, lay cobblestone, or put bricks down?

Moscow, 1860

We see a similar situation for Moscow in 1860. It is an empty city with muddy streets.

Other cities around the world at this time look similar to St. Petersburg. They are ghost cities with amazing architecture and unpaved roads.

Madrid, 1870s

BURGOS.__1568.__Vista de Burgos tomada desde el Museo provincial. J. Laurent. Madrid.

TOLEDO.—1.—Entrada de Toledo por el puente de Alcántara. J. Laurent. Madrid.

MADRID.—41.—Vista general de la puerta del Sol. J. Laurent. Madrid.

Prague, 1856

Helsinki, 1860s

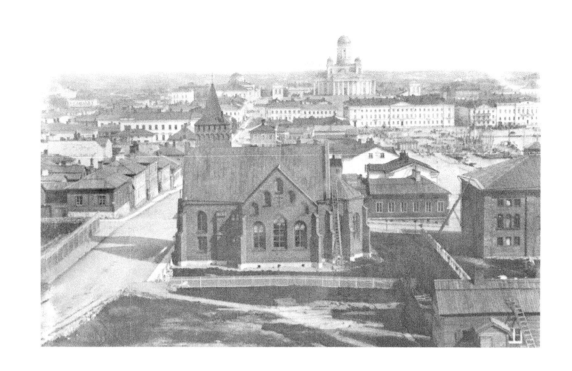

Copenhagen, Denmark 1840s

Bombay, 1850

Notice how the same type of architecture with columns and bell towers can be found in the East as well as the West.

Malta,Italy 1880

Dresden 1860s

Rio in Brazil 1860s

Turku, Finland, 19th Century

Toronto, Canada 1860s

Athens, Greece

Cape Town, 1870s

Were cities abnormally empty and muddy during this time period? Do these cities seem like ghost cities which once held larger populations in the past?

Mainstream journalists say these photographs appeared empty because the shutter on old cameras moved too slowly to capture people. Meaning, the shutter on the camera had to remain open for a certain length of time to properly expose the plate to light. Early daguerreotype images required an exposure of around twenty minutes. But by the early 1840s, it had been reduced to about twenty seconds.   At this speed, moving people may appear as faint smudges in a photograph. Parked horses and carts might still appear though.   The cities still seem too empty for mud flood theorists to dismiss. They say we should see more photographic evidence of people occupying these cities. We should see more faint smudges of moving people, more parked horses, and more evidence of daily commerce such as fruit stands, newspaper stands, or people sitting idle.

Expert photographers debunking the mud flood theory might argue that photographers liked to take pictures in the early morning when they had the streets to themselves. However, not every picture was taken in the morning. It is easy to observe the shadows in photographs to predict whether it is mid-day or morning/evening.

This research of examining old historical photographs of cities can easily be replicated independently on the internet. Pick a city, and google its earliest historical photographs. What do you find? Were the pictures in this book 'cherry picked' to appear empty, or are they a fair representative of the earth during this time?

The 1880s: Horse-and-Buggy People Inherit Advanced Architecture

Mud Flood theorists claim that cities in the 1860s appear empty and muddy, but that cities in the 1880s appear bustling with life. The photographs in the 1880s and 1890s seem to show primitive people with horse-and-buggies inheriting advanced architecture .

The advanced architecture in these photographs does not seem to match its people. We see beautiful old cities with enormous, great buildings in old historical photographs. These buildings all seem to have the same intricate neoclassical architectural style. This great architecture stands in direct contrast with an underdeveloped civilization with horse-drawn carriages on mud roads without advanced technology.

Why did people seem so primitive with their horses and buggies when they occupied cities in historical photographs? Why do their buildings seem so advanced in contrast? Why are people so small in comparison with the buildings?

The Opera House, Paris, 1890

Saint-Laurent's, Paris, between 1890 and 1900

The Royal Exchange, between 1890 and 1900, London.

People Moving into Advanced Cities With Covered Wagons?

Some photographs almost appear as if people are moving into vacant cities with their covered wagons, ready to occupy old, empty buildings. Do these photographs show primitive people of a modern era inheriting buildings built from a previous, more advanced era?

London Bridge, 1890s

Atlanta Wagon Train, 1860s

Berlin Wagon Train, 1857

A Tale of Two Cities: Newer, Crooked Construction Alongside Advanced Architecture.

Often you can see newer, primitive wooden shacks built alongside older neoclassical architecture. These buildings seem less-developed and refined and would be more fitting for a horse and buggy culture. Did people stop building neoclassical buildings during this time period? Perhaps the buildings were built better in the past and humans lost this building technology. Why would people build new shacks when huge, beautiful buildings seem empty behind them? Maybe this housing was built by a slave class excluded from the cities.

New and old: the recently completed Uspenski Cathedral is surrounded by a shanty-town of tumbledown cottages in this image from 1868. Photo: Hoffers Eugen, Helsinki City Museum / CC BY-ND 4.0

Helsinki, 1868

Banks of the Bièvre River at the Bottom of the rue des Gobelins, Paris c. 1862, Charles Marville

London 1875

London, Crooked Buildings at the back of St Bartholomew's, Smithfield

Paris in 1877.

Charles Marville, "Top of the rue Champlain, View to the Right (Twentieth Arrondissement)" (1877-78), albumen silver print from glass negative

Are We Truly Advancing as a Society?

Supposedly people did not have the electric drill until the 1950s, but managed to build all this! Yet people still used horse and cart. Perhaps the civilization prior to the horse-and-cart-culture was more advanced and had tools that were forgotten about. Maybe we are not a progressive society. It could be that our civilizations were more advanced in the past. Look at these classic examples of horse and buggies next to amazing neoclassical architecture all around the world in the 19th Century.

Rome, 19th Century
Modern Horse and Cart in Contrast with Ancient Buildings with High Tech

Budapest

Constantinople

Were Wild West Cities Found, or Built in the 19th Century?

Do old aerial photographs of western cities in the US show that they were built before settlers found them?

What if the academic timeline we are given for cities in the western United States is a lie?

Mud Flood theorists claim that the history of US Western Cities is unbelievable. They say it was impossible for small, unskilled frontiersman to build western cities so fast. Cities in the Wild West often had no local building materials and were isolated from railroads and navigable rivers at the time their first buildings were built. Yet, photographs show that citizens somehow built amazing buildings despite these hardships. Mud Flood theorists say America was filled with old-world buildings and structures just like Europe. They claim American history was manufactured, and that a previous civilization with neoclassical architecture occupied the Wild West just like Europe before the Reset Mud Flood.

American History 101

Historians say Columbus discovered America in 1492. Europeans colonized the Eastern United States the 1600s and 1700s. The Midwestern and Western United States remained relatively empty through the early 1800s save for a few Native Americans. Europeans saw most of the United States as a fresh canvas to be filled by Explorers, Cowboys, and Frontiersman. Lewis and Clark mapped out uncharted land between 1804-1806. Their journals described Native American tribes and wildlife, but did not describe ancient architecture such as cathedrals, domed stone buildings, or canals. Fur traders and trappers laid out the Oregon Trail between 1811 to 1840. The Trail was only passable on foot or on horseback.

White settors did not begin building their buildings in the west until after they traversed the Oregon Trail for various reasons. Such as for a gold rush, or to claim new, vacant land. Yet, the earliest photographs of America seem to clash with this narrative. Were cities built before we are told?

San Francisco

Was San Francisco Built too Fast?

San Francisco, once known as Yerba Buena, listed 21 residents in an 1842 census. In 1846, there were under 500 Mormon settlers living on the area of land in what we now call San Francisco. Between 1848 and 1849 with the start of the California Gold Rush, the population increased from 10,000 people to 25,000 people.

In 1851, San Francisco looked like this. Does it seems impossible for a small population of 25,000 to build San Francisco to this extent within two years of arriving? Where are the construction cranes in this photograph?

San Francisco 1851

American frontiersmen allegedly constructed these new cities from scratch using local materials. According to school textbooks, San Francisco should have been a shanty town. Most 49ers traveled along the Oregon Trail. We are told that San Francisco was a jungle of tents and wood shacks built by unskilled people using local materials. However, the actual photographs of San Francisco stand in direct contrast with the storybook version of a gold miners' primitive shanty town.

Did the 49ers really build San Francisco? How do you account for the fact that the buildings may have already been there before most of the population arrived?

San Francisco's Empty Streets and Missing People

San Francisco 1878

San Francisco's 1878 panorama photographs depict an eerily empty and deserted city, captured by Eadweard Muybridge from the top of Nob Hill. We are told that San Francisco had a population of 233,000 in 1878. But the photographs seem to say otherwise. There is a complete absence of people and objects in the photographs. San Francisco looks like a ghost town!

Mud flood theorists suggest that San Francisco was an old city and was built before the 1830s. It suffered a mud flood and depopulation event. And these photos were taken after the city was reset and prepared for a new population to arrive after 1878. Mainstream historians dismiss this theory and suggest that the 1878 panorama was taken in the early morning before people began their day. They argue that the city was not actually empty but that the photographer captured a quiet moment before the hustle and bustle of daily life began.

However, mud flood theorists also point to the complete absence of personal belongings around the buildings. There are no window boxes, fruit stands, pieces porch furniture, strollers, or any other freestanding objects to indicate that this city is currently being occupied.

Furthermore, mud flood theorists argue that all these impressive European-style buildings could not have been built in less than thirty years of the city being occupied by gold miners. While it is true that the gold rush brought many immigrants to the city, the construction of such buildings required skilled labor and architects, making it unlikely that miners built them on their own.

The photographs of San Francisco in 1878 definitely appear strange and mysterious. They seem to support the mud flood hypothesis.

46

San Francisco 1878

Phoenix, Arizona

Built from Scratch, or Seeded with Leftover Buildings from a Previous Civilization?

Was Phoenix a brand new city in 1867, or was it parts of a leftover city from a past civilization predating the 1830s?

Historians say that the city of Phoenix was founded in 1867 by a former Confederate soldier named Jack Swilling. Swilling allegedly discovered evidence of old canals from the Hohokam people. These canals fell into ruin after the Hohokam disappeared, but they allegedly built over 500 miles of these canals in the past. Jack Swilling and a group of a few settlors started digging. Swilling's group dug 2 miles of canals by 1868. By the 20th century, Phoenix had over 100 miles of canals. These canals created a potential for agriculture in the region. Large scale agriculture became possible after these canals were revived, and an economy developed around cotton, citrus, and cattle.

Before 1887, builders allegedly used local materials to build the city since Phoenix was located in the middle of the Sonoran Desert. There was no easy way to transport imported materials to Phoenix until its first functioning railroad in July 1887. Phoenix also did not have deep rivers that could be navigated by ships. The only mode to transport heavy materials before 1887 were mule trains, which were expensive.

The City of Phoenix grew rapidly in the late 19th and early 20th centuries, fueled by the arrival of the railroad. The architecture was influenced by Spanish and Anglo-American styles with buildings featuring stucco walls, red tile roofs, and wood shutters. Adobe houses, which are made from a mixture of mud, straw, and water were also common.

But is it possible that the city of Phoenix, Arizona was built before the 1830s, and then suffered a depopulation event? Perhaps our Controllers preserved a few buildings and the extensive infrastructure from the old city to seed a new civilization to inhabit in the 1880s.   The infrastructure included hundreds of miles of old canals that ran through the desert. How else can you explain how a city seemed to be built in the middle of the desert before receiving its railroad in 1887?

Rough Adobe Houses in Phoenix

Most of Phoenix built before the arrival of the railroad in 1887 were rough adobe houses. So we are told.   Phoenix residents constructed these houses with mud reinforced with mesquite, cactus, and rocks. Phillip Darrell Duppa's adobe mud-house is an example of an adobe house allegedly built in the 1870s. The Duppa-Montgomery Adobe House is one of Phoenix's oldest houses. Structures such as these were once all over Phoenix. But they were fragile and melted with the elements.

But is this a fake narrative? Maybe Phoenix was a global city with European-style buildings before a Mud Flood reset. Perhaps mainstream historians are trying to assert the narrative that Phoenix was a new city with rough adobe structures so we do not know that a previous advanced civilization occupied this land.

47

The Phoenix Courthouse

How were Advanced Buildings Constructed in the Middle of the Desert before Railroad?

Builders constructed this old courthouse building in 1884 in the middle of a desert, without a good mode of transporting foreign materials to the building site. There were no railroads, navigable rivers, in 1884, and the Sonoran Desert lacked great building materials. Historians might claim that mule trains transported materials hundreds of miles across wilderness to build structures like this.

Old Courthouse building built in year 1884. But pictured in late 1890s.

Phoenix Bird's Eye Map

Does the Bird's Eye Map of Phoenix 1885 Show Leftover Bits of an Old Advanced City?

Phoenix is depicted in this bird's eye map of Phoenix from 1885. The map shows a small town with a perfect road layout. It shows canals that bring water towards the city in the background. it depicts nice public buildings and private residences. The map does not seem to depict rough, muddy adobe structures that look like a kid's play doh project or a wild west outpost depicted in Hollywood movies.

The city only had about 3,500 residents in 1885, but possessed fully functioning canals, and a few nice brick and stone buildings to fulfill basic functions of government, education, and religion. The County Courthouse and public school house are depicted on the 1885 map in the bottom corners. They certainly do not look like new, primitive adobe structures. This town looks like it has typical brick or stone structure like any old established, global cities in the 19th century.

The Phoenix Insane Asylum

Why Was the Phoenix's Insane Asylum so Enormous and Complex?

The State of Arizona needed an insane asylum, and built this Arizona State Hospital in 1886. This was built a year before Phoenix had a railroad or any good way to import building materials. This enormous building was constructed during a time where Phoenix customarily only had rough adobe buildings made of clay. In 1887, the hospital admitted 61 mental patients at its opening. What an extensive complex! How would the supply chains support getting the materials to build this in the middle of the desert? Why was this one of the first major buildings built for the city?

Starting in 1913, a fire destroyed the original hospital. Fires destroyed a lot of these historical structures that seem too large and intricate for a new city with a small unskilled population. This seems to be the pattern for older buildings that seemed too good to have been built in a new city. They all are often mysteriously destroyed!

Was Phoenix really created with imported materials or mud?

In 1888, the military parade in Phoenix looked like this! This was about a year after Phoenix had its first railroad. Was this city made up of mostly adobe shacks as described in the mainstream historical narrative? Were the power lines constructed from mud as well? How did they build all this before they had a great way to transport materials into the desert? If this is a brand new city, where are all the construction cranes? If the mainstream view on history is correct, building materials would have had to be transported over hundreds of miles by mule trains to construct the city.

Perhaps this city was older than what we are told. It could have experienced a reset, and this parade may be commemorating the emergence of a new civilization akin to the Phoenix rising from the ashes.

Was the Adobe building narrative a cover for a Fiery Disaster Two Resets Back?

The storybook version describes Phoenix as full of rough-adobe-structures made of clay. Settlors were inspired to build adobe buildings by looking at ancient Indian relics, we are told. According to mainstream historians, the pre-1887 buildings looked so crude, that citizens confused them with relics from past centuries. Especially with structures the Hokomon People built.

But what if these ancient Hokomon relics in the desert really were actually ancient buildings from a great civilization that melted in a fiery disaster? What if these buildings were actually made of brick with facing and not actually clay? Maybe historians are trying to sell the idea that everything in Phoenix before 1887 was made with clay to fool us into believing that ancient civilizations were not advanced.

For instance, the ancient Hohokam people allegedly built Casa Grande near Phoenix, complete with a water system. Don't look at the bottom right corner of its west facade and ask why it looks like a regular brick structure covered with a melted facing!! A mainstream historian might explain the brick away by noting that the Bureau of American Ethnology repaired the building in 1891. But it is odd that the brick seems perfectly laid under a melted looking facade.

Side view of the Casa Grande Ruins [48]

Why does Casa Grande have kiln-fired bricks underneath a clay facade?

Swillings Ditch: 250 miles of Canals Fully Functioning in 1885?

The Hohokam Indians built between 250-500 miles of ancient canals in 200 AD, fanning out from the Salt River to irrigate the desert and grow crops. But the Hohokam Indians disappeared. In fact, the name Hohokam is interpreted to mean "those who have vanished" or "those who have gone." For 400 years, the canals endured flash flooding and were cooked by the sun.

A man name Jack Swilling was inspired by these canals, and built more canals in Wickenburg with a team of 15 other men. His popularity grew, and they dug more canals on top of or near the old Hohokam canals that ran east and west just north of the Salt River. The canals delivered much needed water for irrigation and much needed other uses in the growing desert community. It is amazing how this small crew of men built, or re-dug these extensive canals before the town was settled by a mere 3500 citizens. People referred to these waterways as "Swilling's Ditch".

The 1885 Bird's Eye map depicted "Swilling's Ditch" and the canals flowing through the town. How does one downplay hundreds of miles of canals that were dug out before a city was built? Call these canals a "Ditch"!

Salt Lake City

Did Mormons and 49ers Build Salt Lake City From the Ground Up, or Did They Inherit Remnants of a previous civilization?

Salt Lake City has the same type of neoclassical architecture as the rest of the world from our previous period in history, without much difference.

The difference is that Salt Lake City is not much more than a hundred years old. Salt Lake City is a relatively new city established shortly after San Francisco. The feasibility of building out such an advanced, highly developed city in such a short period of time without advanced technology seems impossible.

It's one thing to see advanced, intricate neoclassical architecture in Europe, the Middle East, and other parts of the globe where this style would fit into the historical narrative. But when this neoclassical style comprises most of a city built out in less than 50 years by a people who arrived in horse, wagon, oxen, and the clothes on their back it seems unbelievable. Especially when the population was so small and had no modern machinery or massive manpower.

Originally, the Shoshone, Paiute, Goshute and Ute Native American tribes inhabited the Salt Lake Valley. Brigham Young led the first non Native-Americans into the Salt Lake Valley. His group of 143 men, three women and two children "founded" Salt Lake City on July 24, 1847. The California Gold Rush brought many people through the city on their way to seek fortunes. The Congress organized the Utah Territory in 1850.

Salt Lake City in 1850

Salt Lake City was still a wilderness outpost before 1870. Its first railroad was not completed until 1869. Its population was 12,000. Salt Lake is an arid mountain desert, though it does have a few trees and large stone quarries.

Does this map show a wild west town organically built from the ground up in 20 years? Or does the map show a few buildings and infrastructure left from a previous civilization to seed the next one?

Mud Flood theorists argue that the city seems perfectly laid out. Were Mormans expert land topographers and cartographers? Also, when a people organically form a city and build it from scratch, they start with shanty shacks made of timber or mud huts. A new city with a population of 12,000 people might not construct an enormous structure like the Salt Lake Temple before it has a chance to grow.

SALT LAKE CITY
UTAH TERRITORY

Salt Lake City's Tabernacle

How was the Tabernacle Built Before Railroad? Was the Tabernacle a Blimp Hangar?

The Mormans built this unique looking Tabernacle. Historians want to date this structure's construction after Salt Lake City had the railroad in 1869, but the exact years of construction conflict depending on the historian you read. Some say the Tabernacle was constructed between 1864 and 1867. [49] Others say between 1863 to 1875.[50] Still other historians say the Tabernacle was completed in 1870.[51] Perhaps they're doctoring the story so it looks like it was built after the railroad arrived.

Henry Grow, a Bridge Builder, designed and built this tabernacle to span as broad an area as he could without using interior supports. He constructed the roof like a lattice bridge, which vertically distributes the very heavy weight of the roof and keeps the sandstone buttresses in alignment.

This Salt Lake Tabernacle is famous for its superior acoustics. Its builders designed the tabernacle so that all attendees could hear the speaker's voice from wherever they sat. The Tabernacle features an enormous organ.

A bizarre aerial view of the tabernacle in the 1930s shows how the Tabernacle Choir has "Salt Lake Airport" painted on top of it. Mainstream historians say that airplanes kept getting lost, and a sign with an arrow had to point out the location of the airport. Some Mud Flood theorists believe the tabernacle looks like an old blimp or airship hanger, and it was understood as such in the 1930s.

Airships were popular in the previous civilization. Maybe the Tabernacle was originally built as a hippodrome to store a large blimp since it had no interior supports or columns.   Perhaps it was located next to an airport for convenience to its airship travelers. Why would Mormons take such care in building fantastic temples, only to let an airport paint a sign on top of their roof for convenience? No one spray paints a sacred structure for use as a billboard sign. Perhaps this unique structure was an old blimp hippodrome leftover from a previous civilization, and was repurposed as a Mormon temple.

US Navy Blimp over Hangar, Photo from US Navy

.

The Salt Lake Assembly Hall

Why did Salt Lake Require So Much Religious Space for a Very Small Start-up Town?

The Salt Lake Assembly Hall was constructed for The Church of Jesus Christ of Latter-day Saints (LDS Church) in 1877 and could hold 1400 people.

It seems that residents in a new city would not have this many resources to put towards a gorgeous religious building. In 1880, the population of Salt Lake was around 20,000 and had very few buildings. Salt Lake City was a mere wild west outpost at this point.

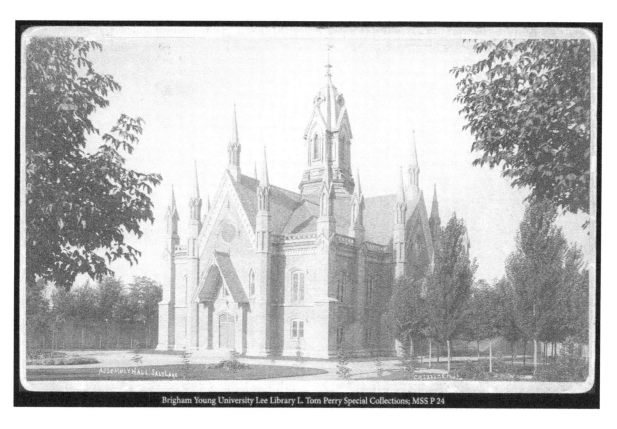

Brigham Young University Lee Library L. Tom Perry Special Collections; MSS P 24

The Amazing Salt Lake Temple

How was this Built when Salt Lake was still a Wild West Outpost?

The construction of the Salt Lake Temple, an enormous structure built by Mormon pioneers between 1853 and 1893, raises questions for some about its origins. Mud Flood Theorists wonder whether the temple was actually constructed during a previous population peak and "founded," "completed," and "dedicated" to modern civilization after a Reset. They point to supposed inconsistencies in the construction photographs of the temple and the logistics of building such a massive structure in a new city with a small population.

The stones used to construct the Salt Lake Temple were huge, weighing between 2,500 and 5,600 pounds, and it would have required a significant infrastructure to quarry, cut, transport, polish, and assemble them. However, Salt Lake City did not have a railroad until 1870, and most of the population were likely unskilled pioneers engaged in food production and domestic work. Additionally, it seems that essential buildings, such as homes, farms, shops, schools, banks, and government buildings, would have needed to be built before a gigantic religious temple.

Here is a picture of the construction of Salt Lake Temple in 1881. We see a crane on top of the Temple. This passes for a construction photo to most people quickly glancing at it. But upon closer look, does this photo really look believable?

Salt Lake Temple Construction: Real or Photoshopped?

Mud Flood theorists say construction photographs during the reset period are often photoshopped. They believe the Salt Lake Temple construction photos were photoshopped because the Temple was built in a previous time when the City had a larger population. They note that the bottom floors looked fully built and aged in the construction photographs. It looks as if an artist doctored the photo by merely cutting the top of the building off. The edge on the top of the building seems jagged, as if it were roughly cut out by scissors. The artist drew in fake shadow-people to complete the effect. The ground looks undisturbed. The bottom of the Temple looks completed before the top is even framed out. The figures on top of the building look drawn-in.

Are these photos proof that this building was older than what we are told? Was the Salt Lake Temple built in the peak of a previous advanced civilization?

Photoshop Shadow Drawings on Salt Lake Temple "Photo"

Perhaps a much larger, skilled population was required to build a huge, beautiful stone building like the Salt Lake Temple. Salt Lake City had between 6,157-20,000 people between 1850-1880, and most of the people were unskilled Morman pioneers. Forty seven percent of Americans in the 1870s were farmers. Half of the population consisted of women who did not traditionally do construction work. As Salt Lake City did not have any railroads until 1870, it seems that much of its population would be dedicated to food production and domestic work. A new city built from the ground up may need essential buildings built before a gigantic religious temple, such as homes, farm buildings, shops, schools, banks, and government buildings.

Here is a primitive wagon train on its way to the temple dedication in 1893. Riding next to high tech, such as trolleys and amazing architecture. Perhaps they are getting ready to settle in their inherited structures in Salt Lake!

Were Salt Lake Temple's Construction Photographs Photoshopped?

Quarries in Salt Lake City

According to the mainstream narrative, The Salt Lake Temple's granite blocks were quarried from nearby Little Cottonwood Canyon, which is located about 20 miles southeast of Salt Lake City.

The granite blocks were quarried using hand tools such as hammers, chisels, and wedges. The process involved first identifying a suitable location for a quarry, then using hand tools to cut channels around the sides of the granite blocks to loosen them from the surrounding bedrock. The blocks were then lifted out of the quarry using a combination of pulleys, ropes, and brute strength. Transporting the granite blocks from the Little Cottonwood Canyon quarries to the Salt Lake Temple site, which is located in downtown Salt Lake City, was a major logistical challenge. At the time of the temple's construction in the mid-19th century, there were no roads or railways leading from the quarries to the city, and transportation methods were limited to horse-drawn wagons and sleds.

The quarrying process was a labor-intensive and time-consuming endeavor, and it took several years to quarry and transport the thousands of granite blocks needed for the Salt Lake Temple.

Mud flood theorists believe the mainstream narrative is impossible. And that this Temple was constructed in an ancient time before reset when there was technology and infrastructure to make quarrying and transporting these granite blocks feasible.

The Great Saltair

By 1912, Temple Square looked like this.

The Great Saltair was a recreational and entertainment center located on the southern shore of the Great Salt Lake, just outside Salt Lake City, Utah. It was built in 1893 when the population of Salt Lake City was only approximately 53,000 people. The building was supported by more than 2,000 wooden pilings, driven deep into the lake's bedrock to provide a solid foundation for the structure. The Great Saltair served as a destination for tourists and locals alike, featuring a large dance hall, an amusement park with rides and attractions, and a massive saltwater swimming pool. It was a grand and iconic structure, designed to resemble a Moorish palace with its unique architecture and grandeur. The Great Saltair had a saltwater pool, which was the largest of its kind in the world at the time. The pool contained over 2.5 million gallons of water from the Great Salt Lake and was surrounded by white sand beaches.

The construction of the Great Saltair would have been a challenging and arduous task, requiring the labor of hundreds of workers over a period of several years. The building materials had to be transported to the site by train, and then hauled by horse-drawn wagons to the lake's shore. The pilings had to be driven deep into the lake's bedrock, which required specialized equipment and skilled laborers. Of course, most modern people today do not think of the logistics of constructing such a large structure with only 53,000 people in a new city. Did a population this size really possess the talent and skill to build such a structure?

The Great Saltair strangely burnt down on April 22, 1925. Perhaps this building needed to be taken down to hide evidence that older buildings were better.

Does Salt Lake City Predate the 1830s?

This is what a panorama of Salt Lake City looked like in 1913. Does this panorama resemble an old, European style city with a large infrastructure capable constructing numerous intricate, advanced neoclassical buildings? Or a very new city less than fifty years old that built many of its first buildings by dragging materials across miles and miles of land with horse and cart?

By 1913, Salt Lake City had a population of around 100,000 people. It was a growing and bustling city. The panorama showed its skyline dominated by the spires and towers of the Mormon Temple and Tabernacle, which were the city's most iconic landmarks. The panorama displayed a city that was rapidly growing and expanding. The streets were filled with people, cars, and horse-drawn carriages, and the buildings ranged from old Victorian-era homes to modern skyscrapers. The city's downtown area was a hub of activity, with shops, restaurants, theaters, and other businesses lining the streets. Beyond the downtown area, the panorama shows a mix of residential neighborhoods, industrial areas, and open spaces. The city was surrounded by mountains, and many of the neighborhoods were located on hillsides.

Salt Lake City is similar to San Francisco. Both cities have pictures depicting fifty years of growth. This growth seems as built out in the same fine detail as the most beautiful cities in the world.

Mud flood theorists say cities cannot grow this fast with such few residents. And that cities do not grow like this organically - starting with the best buildings first. Perhaps the older photographs of Salt Lake City are just depicting remnants saved from a previous civilization to seed the next one.

.

Neoclassical style in America?

One peculiar thing you can observe in old American photographs is architecture with a neoclassical style. You see columns, copper or gold domes, obelisks, obelisks, cathedrals, bell towers, and Greek and Roman-style statues.

In school, we are taught the narrative that pioneers built log cabins and cowboys constructed make-do shanty towns. Yet, when we look at the actual photographs of 19th century America, we see Roman-style aqueducts, fountains, and arches.

Piedmont Park in Atlanta, Georgia, 1895

Why would Americans in the 18th and 19th centuries build with this neoclassical architectural style? The official story line is that a lot of buildings were built in the Richardsonian Romanesque style. This style of Romanesque Revival architecture was named after the American architect Henry Hobson Richardson. Other terms for this style or Renaissance, Revival, or Classical. Well, that Henry Hobson Richardson was really busy!! Mansions, buildings, city halls – all built that way in Old America because of that guy!

How come all this architecture is found in so many cities around the world.all built in exactly the same style. And it's the same style we can't duplicate today! Podcasters like Max Igan remark that all our buildings today seem so temporary and so ugly compared to these glorious buildings of the past. And they knocked down a lot of the older buildings… what for?

Interestingly, people often seek ancient architecture in other countries, assumign that cathedrals can only be found in Europe. But if you look take a closer look at your own town, and you're aware of the mud flood happening, you might discover beautiful buildings that have bene overlooked. Your own town hall, capital, cathedral, or other buildings may have been built before a mud flood.

***

The academic timeline of colonists arriving in America and the mainstream historical narrative are presented to us, but what if these timelines are inaccurate?

What if we examine history through our own eyes instead of solely relying on textbooks? We may discover an alternative story.

Perhaps Wild West cities were not founded in the 1840s out of nowhere but were instead previously existing neoclassical-style cities that were advanced and densely populated. Intricate architecture may be evidence of their existence. It's possible that remnants of these cities and their infrastructure were preserved to give rise to a new era.

Did Columbus actually colonize America? How can we explain the presence of beautiful buildings before the majority of the population arrived? As the saying goes, new cities are often built upon the bones of old ones.

Australia

Does Australia have a Faked Timeline?

We are given an academic timeline of Christopher Columbus discovering America, and Captain Cook landing in Australia. We are given a mainstream historical narrative complete with illustrations and colorful firsthand accounts. However, what if these mainstream narratives are false?

According to the Mud Flood theorists, many of the buildings in Australia were already present before the earliest known European populations were said to arrive, challenging the established narrative.

The History of Australia: Prisoners and Gold Miners

Mainstream historians tell us that Lieutenant James Cook was the first European to chart the eastern coast of Australia and make a detailed map of the region in 1770. In 1788, Britain declared Australia as a British colony when a fleet of ships led by Captain Arthur Phillip arrived at Sydney Cove in what is now New South Wales.

Britain used Australia as a penal colony to relieve overcrowding in British prisons. Britain transported convicts to this distant land where they could be put to work. In the following decades, more convicts were sent to Australia, and free settlers established farms, businesses, and towns. The colony expanded gradually, with new settlements established in Tasmania, South Australia, Victoria, Queensland, and Western Australia.

In the 1850s, significant quantities of gold were discovered in Victoria, New South Wales and other parts of Australia. The discovery of gold led to a surge in population as people flocked to the goldfields in search of riches. The gold rush also brought new technologies, infrastructure, and economic growth to Australia, which helped shape the country's development in the decades that followed.

Autonomous parliamentary democracies were established throughout the six British colonies in the mid-19th century. New South Wales, Victoria, Queensland, South Australia, Western Australia, and Tasmania united to form the Commonwealth of Australia. The colonies voted by referendum to unite in a federation in 1901, and modern Australia came into being.

Melbourne:

Beautiful Buildings Constructed by Unskilled Convicts and Gold Miners?

Charles's Netteton was a photographer in Australia who took many of the historic photographs we have of Australia today, especially of Melbourne.

The population of Melbourne was extremely small compared to the extent of its build out between the years 1850-1880. In 1851, the City of Melbourne had a population of only 23,000 individuals. However, the municipality's population surged from 37,000 in 1861 to 55,000 in 1871, and subsequently reached 66,000 in 1881 and 73,000 in 1891.

Thankfully, this small population of 35,000 had a beautiful post office! You can see that one lone guy out there, waiting to deliver a handwritten letter to a special someone.

Melbourne Post Office, built in 1859, photographed by Charles Nettleton in 1868

Following a Royal Commission in 1854, the building of a new Asylum at Kew began in 1864. Kew is a suburb of Melbourne. Asylums for the insane were of such enormous importance in this time period, that citizens dedicated the most beautiful buildings for this purpose! Convicts and Gold Miners were talented construction workers, but poor landscapers. They had trouble making anything grow on the lawn.

Asylum at Kew

Melbourne in 1867.

This is Bourke Street looking west from Spring Street, 1861. Showing an empty, muddy city.

Melbourne Government House, 1870

Melbourne Hospital 1870, constructed between 1846-1848

The Melbourne Bank of Australia was built in 1878.

The Oriental Bank in Melbourne was built in 1858.

Alfred Hospital, Melbourne, in 1870. Construction began in 1869.

This photograph was taken by Charles Nettleton 14 May 1885 showing workmen digging the moat around Fort Queenscliff. The Fort was constructed in 1860. Is this building older than what we are told?

Sydney: A large City Erected Overnight

Like every Australian City, Sydney began with convicts. Gold rushes followed. It seems that gold miners and convicts would have been equally unskilled at quarrying and assembling stone for neoclassical buildings. But they defied everyone's expectations! Sydney was allegedly in the middle of nowhere when constructed.

1860 Sydney: Advanced Architecture, Empty and Muddy

Pictures in the late 1850s and early 1860s of Sydney show beautiful buildings in an empty muddy city.

St. Andrews Cathedral, 1860

Herald Office, Pitt Street, Sydney, 1860 -1863

George Street, 1858

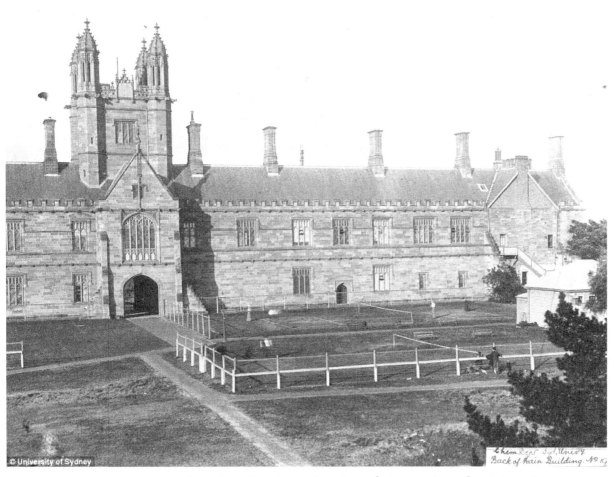

Sydney University Quadrangle, site of Australia's first tennis courts

ca. 1860

Sydney Observatory 1860

University of Sydney 1877
(Looks like Grass is finally taking root!)

1900 Sydney: Horse and Buggies Move In!

The City is now fully Reset, and ready for the Horse and Buggy people!!! Time to move in!!

Vintage glass plate images of streets from Sydney City (1900s)

Streets of Sydney City 1900s.jpg

George Street looking south 1900s – compare with the photograph from 1858.

2863. VICTORIA MARKETS.
KERRY. PHOTO. SYDNEY.

This is the Queen Victorian Building and Victorian Markets 1900s.   This Romanesque Revival building was constructed between 1893 and 1898 and is 98 feet wide by 620 feet long. The domes were built by Ritchie Brothers, a steel and metal company that also built trains, trams and farm equipment.

The Palace Emporium was erected 1905

Streets of Sydney City (1900s)
Nice Statues! Convicts and Gold Rushees love them! Fits right in with their style.

Panorama of Sydney Town Hall and Queen Victoria Building, 1904 by Melvin Vaniman

Australia was allegedly populated by unskilled convicts and Gold Rushers in the 1800s. We are to believe that these people were incredible stone masons and somehow built all these beautiful buildings using hand tools. It is amazing that criminals and gold rushers built these quarries and erected these buildings using primitive cranes, but hid all the cranes right before the cities were photographed.   These buildings were settled in by the "horse and buggy people" shortly thereafter. Did the few people who lived in Sydney quarry these blocks and build all these buildings, or were the buildings already there from a previous civilization, and modern people just moved into it.

Did Columbus colonize America? Did Cook colonize Australia? How do you account for the fact that the buildings may have already been there before most of the population arrived? Perhaps Australia's modern civilization is living on the bones of a previous civilization.

Buried Buildings

Do buildings with partially buried windows and doors indicate there was a mud flood in the past?

Is there evidence to suggest that a mud flood occurred in the past and caused buildings to be partially buried? Supporters of the Mud Flood theory point to old buildings as evidence of a global mud flood event. These buildings have their first floors buried about 6 to 12 feet underground, including windows and doors. The theory suggest that during the flood, several meters of mud washed in and buried the ground levels of buildings worldwide. However, mainstream history does not mention such an event.

Why do we not hear about any such event in our history books?

It is not just the foundations of the buildings that are buried, but the windows and doors. Many buildings have windows at ground level.

Many buildings also have windows partially below ground level, as in the photograph below. These buildings often have a metal fence that surrounds the sunken area in front of the basement, called a "basement well" or "window well". Perhaps these buildings survived a mud flood that buried these windows, and the surviving population had to dig these windows out!

Architects argue that this partially-buried design was common in the 19th century when basement spaces were used for storage or as living quarters for servants. The grating provided ventilation and natural light to the lower level while preventing people from falling in.

However, supporters of the Mud Flood theory claim that this explanation is unlikely, as many historic buildings have bricked up windows below ground floor, which would be illogical to build. They believe that people did not purposefully build windows or front doors below ground that would open to face dirt, just to brick them up later. Many people have found windows below ground that were bricked in after the supposed flooding event on YouTube.

Many buildings have first floor entrances that are raised from the ground level. As if the mud flood buried the first floor, and the second floor had to become the new main floor.

Some historical buildings have steps leading down to entrances below ground level. Possibly because new mud was deposited over the old ground level.

Why are there so many windows and doors below ground level? Were they old style-basements? Supporters of the Mud Flood argue that building basements would have been hard work during a time before tractors or steam shovels. Large powered excavation machines, such as backhoes and front-end loaders, were not available at the time these buildings were constructed. Geologists claim that mud can deposit in a city over time, but supporters argue that erosion is as likely to occur naturally, and mud does not usually deposit that quickly over a couple of centuries. Although mud flood theorists content that people had ancient technology that assisted the construction of buildings, they claim building basements was not the style before the mud flood occurred.

There are also buildings with complete windows and floors that seem like they were excavated during a re-grading project.[53]

For example, there is a debate between mud flood theorists and mainstream historians regarding The St. Mary Magdalene Catholic Church in Omaha, Nebraska. According to mud flood theorists, the church was buried more than 20 feet with mud, which forced the new inhabitants to raise the front door to its current location. Mainstream historians claim that the church underwent a renovation in the 1960s, during which the original structure was underpinned to create a new floor and entrance 20 feet above the ground level.

The debate between mud flood theorists and mainstream historians extends to many other buildings, where the excavation of land around them raises questions about the origin of their lower floors. Some believe the lower floors were newly built, while others argue they were already there and merely excavated due to road regrading or flooding issues.

Do Underground Cities show evidence of a Mud Flood?

Those who believe in the mud flood believe that there was so much mud deposited in certain areas, that it required an entire town to be raised up a full story. Often they use historical pictures of road regrading projects as evidence that a mud flood occurred.

Some cities have entire sections underground. For example, the Seattle Underground is a network of underground passageways and basements in the Pioneer Square neighborhood of Seattle, Washington, United States. After the Great Seattle Fire of June 6, 1889, the town's streets were regraded one to two stories higher. Buildings at Seattle Underground were located at ground level when the city was built in the mid-19th century but fell into disuse after the streets were elevated. In recent decades, they have become a tourist attraction, with guided tours taking place around the area. The Seattle Underground Tour takes tourists into the forgotten world of Seattle as it was in 1900.

54

Chattanooga also has four streets with first floors underground. There is no record of these buildings being built. The official story was that the Tennessee River flooded several times at the end of the 19th and begin of the 20th century. Therefore, the city started to raise the street level. The shops and bars of the former ground level, which were now in the basement, were moved up to the new ground level and the lower level was abandoned.

Were Chattanooga and Seattle old cities that were built before a mud flood?

Repopulation in the 1880s

Was the World Repopulated in the 1880s after a Depopulation-Reset?

According to Mud Flood Theorists, a worldwide catastrophic event in the 1830s led to a depopulation-reset, followed by a sudden repopulation of the world in the 1880s. They wonder if there was an intentional repopulation of the earth in the 1880s. They cite empty city photographs prior to the 1880s and a sudden boom in population by 1900 as evidence for their theory.

Mainstream historians acknowledge this boom in the 1880s, but attribute it to an increase in life expectancy, as advances in medical technology and sanitation led to a decline in mortality rates. This, combined with improved living standards, led to a significant increase in population growth. Census estimates show a decrease in the average number of children born to an American woman from seven to eight in 1800 to about 3.5 in 1900, and that this decline is due to the Industrial Revolution improving survival rates of children in previous centuries.

Mud Flood theorists question why human populations did not experience this significant growth until the Industrial Age, and argue that if humans had been around for 26,000 years under the theory of evolution, there should be a much larger population. Similarly, if humans had been around for 5,000 years under the Bible theory, the population should also be higher. They propose the possibility of an intentional repopulation of the earth in the 1880s, utilizing methods such as orphan trains, foundling homes, inexpensive boarding schools, cloning, and incubator babies offered for adoption at World's Fairs.

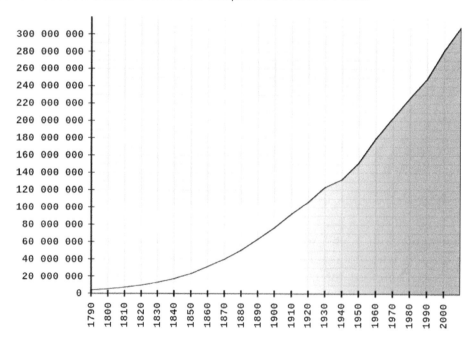

US Census Population Graph from 1790 [55]

Incubator Babies

Mud Flood Theorists believe Incubator Baby displays at World's Fairs are bizarre. They believe they may have been connected to human cloning and repopulation during the late 1800s.

During the late 1800s and early 1900s, physician Martin Couney held incubator exhibits at World's Fairs and amusement parks to demonstrate the efficacy of infant incubators throughout the US and Europe. At his exhibits, Couney demonstrated that isolating premature infants in an incubator ward could significantly decrease premature infant mortality and increased the use of incubators in the US.

At the Exposition in Berlin, Couney held an exhibit called the Kinderbrutanstalt (child hatchery) to demonstrate the effectiveness of infant incubators. Upon arriving in Berlin, Couney obtained six premature infants from the director of the Charité hospital, Rudolph Virchow. All six infants were expected to die. Couney kept all six infants in incubators in a pavilion at the Exposition. Over a hundred thousand visitors paid to see the infants. All six infants survived for the two months of the Exposition. Following the Berlin Exposition, Couney coordinated infant incubator displays in London, Nebraska, and New York for over three decades. Couney treated more than 8,000 premature infants, over 6,500 of whom lived.

Seattle 1909 World's Fair incubator babies

Large Foundling Homes in the 19th Century

The "Lost Generation" consisted of people born between 1883 and 1900. This Generation entered early adulthood during World War I. Historians allegedly refer to this Generation as "Lost" to describe the disoriented, wandering, directionless spirit of many of the war's survivors in the early postwar period. However, perhaps this Generation was lost because many were born as orphans or were abandoned!

Mud Flood Theorists believe there were too many Foundling Homes and Orphans in proportion to the Population in the 19th Century. New cities in the United States at that time had small populations with very large orphanages. There were over 64 large orphanages that were founded in the UK during the 19th century.

This girl's orphanage and school was established in 1856 by six Sisters of Charity nuns from Emmitsburg, Maryland

Los Angeles Orphan Asylum, 1900

     Most buildings designated for Orphan Asylums seem huge. It is almost impossible to establish how many orphans existed in the 19th Century, as good records were not kept, or were lost.

     Why were there such large orphanages? According to mainstream historians, many children would lose one or both their parents before coming of age in societies where people married early, had many children, and experienced a high death rate in young adulthood,

     Some of these children were not technically orphans, but were abandoned by their parents. There were a series of laws passed in the 1800s making it almost impossible for unwed mothers to keep their babies. The 1833 Poor Law Reformation introduced bastardy clauses that shifted the entire responsibility for the illegitimate child onto the mother. A lot of social stigma was placed on unwed mothers. Many were placed in work houses. Advertisements for adoption or nurse care became popular in newspapers. Most children of unwed mothers were left with orphanages, asylums, convent schools, and workhouses. All children taken into these institutions were given entirely new identities. They were provided with shelter, food, and clothing temporarily and then sent off to workhouses or another location.

     Mud Flood theorists believe that perhaps some of these children were taken away from adults who survived the mud flood and were placed in large mental asylums. Other theorists surmise that people were bred artificially, and given the false narrative that they were orphans.

The dining hall of the Alexandra Orphanage on Maitland Park

Stoke Orphanage, 1892

Orphans in Literature

Many works of literature feature orphans. 19th Century literary works featuring orphans include Olive Twist, David Copperfield, Pip Pirrip, Jane Eyre, Heathcliff, Catherine Earnshaw, Jude Fawley and Kim. Other works like Les Miserables feature children whose parents abandoned them. This theme continues in modern literature. Such as Harry Potter, The Secret Garden, Anne of Green Gables, Tom Sawyer, Little Orphan Annie, and Ballet Shoes.

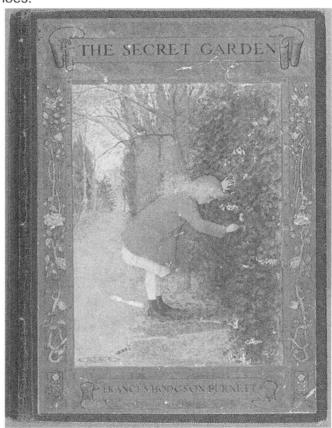

Literary experts say literary works often feature orphans because being an orphan creates great drama. An orphan is a character out of place, forced to make his or her own home in the world. Each novel featuring an orphan will describe the efforts of an ordinary individual to navigate his or her way through the trials of life.

Mud Flood theorists say orphans are featured in literature because they made up a large percentage of the population in the 1880s. If human history is filled with cycles of growth, death, and reset, then a period of repopulation may follow each reset. This period of repopulation would be filled with clones, orphans or 'lost children'.   Maybe all people have orphans in their recent ancestry, yet this history is buried, downplayed, or covered up. Being an orphan is part of our human psyche.

Child Labor:

Was Child Labor Necessary Because There were so Few Adults?

After the reset, there was a generation full of orphans and abandoned children that later became child laborers. Maybe children had to do the work because there were not enough adults around. Why do we see so many 19th century photographs of orphans in workhouses? Why are these children working with machinery created for adult use? Were there not enough adults during this time to carry out this work?

Mainstream historians claim that in 1870, only 1 out of every 8 children was employed. More than 1 in 5 children were employed in 1900. American children worked in large numbers in mines, glass factories, textiles, agriculture, canneries, home industries, and as newsboys, messengers, bootblacks, and peddlers. In the latter part of the nineteenth century, many labor unions and social reformers advocated aggressively for state and local legislation to prevent extreme child labor. By 1900, their efforts had resulted in state and local legislation designed to prevent extreme child labor.

Child Miners

Oyster Shuckers

Orphan Trains:

Our Odd History.

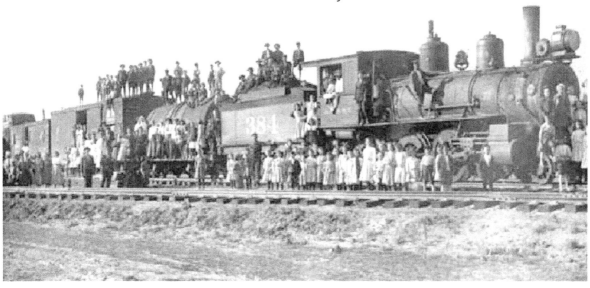

Mud Flood Theorists believe the existence of Orphan Trains is very strange.

The Orphan Train Movement was a welfare program that transported abandoned children from crowded cities to rural areas. The movement began in Europe. The Napoleonic Wars, cholera epidemics, potato famine, and civil war all produced orphans needing a home. Europeans migrated to America, especially New York City. Charities in eastern cities of the United States began to seek foster homes in rural areas of the Midwest. There were also 100,000 children sent to Australia, 100,000 children sent to New Zealand, and 100,000 children sent to Africa

The orphan trains in the United States operated between 1854 and 1929. They re-located about 250,000 children. The founders of the Orphan Train movement claimed that these children were orphaned, abandoned, abused, or homeless. Mainstream historians believe that these were children of new immigrants and the children of the poor and destitute families living in these cities.

Mud Flood Theorists believe the existence of Orphan Trains is very peculiar. Where did these charities obtain all these homeless children? Does it make sense that these children were found in rural areas, re-organized in urban areas, then sent back to rural areas? Why aren't these orphan trains covered in mainstream history books? The official story claims that the Napoleonic Wars, cholera epidemics, the Potato famine, and Civil Wars created orphans. And that working women often dropped their children off at orphanages if they had no day care.

Orphan Trains of the 19th Century

Cabbage Patch Babies

Some proponents of the Mud Flood theory believe that the babies featured in Baby Incubators at World's Fairs may have somehow been bred in Machines, and perhaps our species is 'owned 'by something else. They believe many 19th Century postcards showing babies being born in cabbages allude to cloning or breeding programs for humans during this time.   Apparently, hundreds of 19th Century postcards featured babies being born from cabbages or flowers. They go from cute, to creepy, odd, and disturbing.

A postcard showing three babies being born of flowers promoted a Baby Incubator Exhibit on the caberets of Montmartre in 1896. A female film director named Alice Guy was allegedly inspired by this incubator exhibit, and made the World's first narrative film called The Fairy of the Cabbages. This original film from 1896 was lost, but the film had two remakes in 1900 and 1902. The 1900 version shows an actress pretending to be a fairy raising multiple babies from cabbages. The film features two live babies and several dolls.

First narrative film in 1900 featuring babies born of cabbages

Mud Flood theorists on the Mind Unveiled Youtube channel do not believe these cabbage patch postcards were merely a silly trend. They believe something is very significant about these cards since there are thousands of them around, and because the very first narrative film featured cabbage babies.

Many cabbage patch postcards refer to a repopulation push in the 19th century and feature baby-making machines. The postcard below shows cabbage and rose seeds being mixed into a baby-making device..

Refugee Camps for African Americans?

What if the Civil War never happened? Mud Flood theorists take their questioning of history to extreme lengths, even wondering what would have happened if the Civil War never occurred. If the Wild West's history was fabricated, could the Eastern United States' history have also been falsified?

This leads to questions about the true origins of African Americans. Were they really descendants of slaves brought to America and forced to work on plantations, or were they simply cloned in machines and given a fabricated history and identity?

One Mud Flood theory suggests that the Underground Railroad was literally underground. As believers in the theory that tunnels are a means of survival during resets, some speculate that a select group of people were placed in underground tunnels and raised with the idea of escaping slavery. When they emerged from the tunnels, they were instructed to spread a narrative of bondage to freedom for future generations.

Regardless of these wild theories, it is generally accepted that African Americans lived in refugee camps during and after the Civil War. These camps isolated them and provided a different historical narrative for their ancestry.

Group of "contrabands," people who had escaped slavery during the Civil War at Cumberland Landing, Virginia, 1862. Photographer James F. Gibson.

Slabtown, a refugee camp in Hampton, Virginia, now the site of Hampton University.

A camp holding African Americans could hold anywhere from a few hundred to several thousand people. Most people in these camps lived in barracks or fabric tents.Some of the camps were set up by the Union. The first two camps were set up along the coast in Virginia and South Carolina in 1861. Other camps were in Kentucky and Tennessee. More camps were laid along the Mississippi River from New Orleans to St. Louis, Missouri. Officially, they were called "contraband camps," because freed people were considered property confiscated from the South. Conditions in many of the camps were squalid. Disease and food shortages were common.

There were many plantations photographed in the 1860s. Most African Americans worked on these plantations and were taught to identify as freed slaves.

Boarding Schools for Native Americans

Mud Flood theorists believe there was a cover-up of the event, and that a new generation of children was taught a fake history. Boarding schools was one avenue of teaching the next generation a false narrative.

American Indian boarding schools operated in the United States from the mid 17th to the early 20th centuries. Their primary objective was "civilizing" and assimilating Native American children into Euro-American culture. In the process, these schools denigrated Native American culture and made children give up their languages and religion. Perhaps many native Americans were orphans, and were told their parents died of diseases.

Pupils at Carlisle Native Industrial School, Pennsylvania 1900

Religious and Military Schools For Elite Children

Mud Flood theorists believe society is purposefully divided and stratified between classes. During the repopulation period, children groomed for the upper class were placed in elite boarding schools while underclass children were placed in workhouses.

During the 1800s, boarding schools were associated with the ruling class. Religious boarding schools, especially Jesuit ones, prepared future students for careers in diplomacy. Military life was for those of lesser stature. Religious boarding schools kept children busy. Students woke up at 5 a.m., said prayers as they dressed, attended lessons by 6 a.m., ate two meals each day, and finished lessons by 8 p.m. when they went to bed.

Military boarding schools prepared boys for military life. Sons of officers and administrators of the Empire attended boarding school while their parents fulfilled political and military postings overseas. Military boarding schools were known for bad food and beatings from an early age. There was no fresh fruit, no toilets with doors, and no restraint on bullying. While an institution would be illegal today, it was 'character-forming.' in the 19th and early 20th centuries.

West Point cadets 1870

During the 19th century, the United States Military Academy and Westpoint were allegedly responsible for the construction of the bulk of the nation's earliest waterways, infrastructure, harbors, the Washington Monument, and surveys for the future transcontinental railroads. The greatest engineering feat in world history was the Panama Canal completed in 1914 under the direction of Colonel George W. Goethals (Class of 1880), an Army engineer. Of course, Mud Flood theorists believe that a previous civilization was responsible for these engineering feats, and West Point grads simply took credit for them.

West point graduates gained experience and national recognition during the Mexican and antebellum Indian Wars. West Point graduates also dominated the highest ranks in both the Federal and Confederate armies during the Civil War. Graduates such as generals Ulysses S. Grant, William T. Philip Sheridan and hundreds of others served for the Union Army. Another 304 graduates rejected their oath of allegiance to the United States and served in armed rebellion in the Confederate States Army. Regardless of loyalties, West Point graduates provided significant military leadership for both the North and South.

Large Mental Institutions of the 19th Century

Many mud flood theorists believe the ratio of mental hospitals was too large for the population in the 19th century. Just like with orphanages, huge buildings were dedicated for the purpose of housing the mentally ill. These hospitals were fully equipped with tunnels underground. And a full staff of doctors, chefs, handymen, and other workers as if to form a small city.

Mainstream historians say that mental institutions in the 19th century housed a large number of people, and that many people who should not have been there. People were committed to mental institutions for a wide range of reasons, some of which seem silly by today's standards. Women, in particular, were often committed for reasons such as "female hysteria," which was believed to be caused by a wandering womb. Men were often committed for alcoholism or laziness, and children were committed for disobedience or simply being difficult to handle. Poor people were institutionalized because they had no other means of support, and asylums provided food and shelter. These institutions often provided little actual treatment for patients, and many people were subjected to cruel and inhumane conditions.

Mud flood theorists wonder if these lunatic asylums were actually for people who knew too much. Or who refused to go along with the false narrative of fake history.

Central State Hospital (Milledgeville, Georgia)

The Lost Generation

The Lost Generation is a term used for people born between the years 1883-1900. It was coined by the author Gertrude Stein. The name refers to individuals who came of age during the First World War. The term allegedly refers to the disoriented wandering directionless spirit of many war survivors in the postwar period.

However, could this term actually refer to children who seemed to have appear out of nowhere? Perhaps after a mud flood reset, many children had no parents, and were fed lies about their history and origins.

***

A strange occurrence could have happened in the early 19th century which drastically wiped out the population. This reset may have been followed by a period of repopulation, where the older generation taught the new generation a false history.

This resulted in people who were walking in the cities in those times didn't really belong in those cities. They were the Lost Generation. Maybe they literally rediscovered these cities which were built in a past age. Were children deliberately cut off from their origins? Put on orphan trains, workhouses, and boarding schools?

The many emerging "madhouses" creates the suspicion that the people who knew their origins very well and refused to deny it, were institutionalized. That is how they may have dealt with people who knew too much of the truth.

In any case, the 1880s was characterized by a population boom, and large groups of children were raised in public institutions.

The Intentional Destruction of Ancient Cities

*Were Historical Fires, World's Fairs, Wars, and Unexplained Demolitions
Used as Ways to Get Rid of an Ancient Civilization?*

Many Mud Flood Theorists say the Controllers of our Realm intentionally demolished portions of ancient cities using historical fires, World's Fairs, civil wars, and world wars.

Perhaps during a Reset, a new false narrative is created to transition to a new time. A few old buildings are kept to seed the next age. After a new population is viable, some of these old buildings are deemed unnecessary, and the Elite get rid of the excess. If populations are to live in a new age with new building styles, new fashion, and new lifestyles, the old style must go!

Historical Fires in the United States

Were ancient cities intentionally demolished under the guise of Historic Fires?

Many Mud Flood Theorists claim that sections of old ancient cities were intentionally destroyed under the pretext of fires. They believe that part of a "reset" is getting rid of old structures after they're not needed for modern society to sustain itself.

Perhaps the deep state had to prepare for a new Industrial Age. Part of that job was destroying old buildings to make room for modern cities with steel, cube buildings and factories. If incredible old architecture was kept around, people might question the mainstream historical narrative that the past civilization was primitive without technology.

Historical fires of cities in the United States include: Atlanta, GA (1864), Lawrence, MA (1864), Richmond, VA (1865), Kaiser Burnout, TX (1865), Portland, ME (1866), Port Huron, MI (1871), Chicago, IL (1871), Peshtigo, WI (1871), Boston, MA (1872), Thumb Fire, MI (1881), Martha's Vineyard, MA (1883), Charleston Earthquake, SC (1886), Seattle, WA (1889), and Roxbury, MA (1894).

Mainstream historians have an explanation for everyone of these fires. Some funny - like O'Leary's cow who kicked over a lantern in a barn at night in 1871 that started the great Chicago fire. These stories have become part of our national folklore.

Mud flood theorists don't buy the official narrative. They say nothing seems to add up in the photographs of old historic fires. Wooden structures and trees seem to remain intact next to devastated burnt out buildings. Unwanted buildings are completely leveled next to untouched buildings that they wanted to preserve. There seems to be no objects in the buildings taken down by fires, as if the buildings were empty before their demolitions.

Boston Fire of 1872

Was the Boston fire of 1872 an accidental fire which destroyed parts of an inhabited city?
Or was it a deliberate demolition campaign carried out within a deserted city abandoned long ago?

The Boston Fire allegedly broke out on November 9, 1872 and blazed for only around 12 hours. It destroyed a whopping 776 buildings across 65 acres of land in this short length of time. It spread rapidly, creating its own energy or firestorm, due to the tremendous heat generated. Even though many of the buildings in the fire's path were made of stone or brick, the flames were so hot that some structures actually melted. Firefighters subdued the flames by blowing up buildings with Black Gunpowder, to limit the fire's fuel supply. (Really?) The cause of the fire was never determined, but the spread was blamed on the wooden Mansford roofs which were popular in the district

Does this look as if bombs went off, or does this look like a natural organic fire which broke out. How could a fire be so hot that it completely demolishes this brick and stone building?

You can observe a wooden sign and door frame that were left untouched by fire in the debris, while bricks and stones melted and crumbled. Similarly, the building behind the destruction seems to be left untouched. It is a mystery how a fire can be so hot that it causes stones to crumble into a pile like that.

Thank goodness the trees made it!! The fire took the bricks and stones down, but not the trees

Here, there is unburnt wood on top of the debris melted by fire.

In the above photograph, note the lack of possessions, fixtures, or objects in the rubble. Was this a fire in an occupied building? Or a demolition of an empty building?

Some Mud Flood theorists suggest that space weapons like HAARP were used to take down these buildings. They say this is the only way you could have buildings turned to rubble next to trees that were left untouched. Other people simply point to the gunpowder firefighters allegedly used to break the fire's path.

Were Space Weapons Used in Old Historical Fires?

Many Mud Flood theorists compare these historic fires to the recent California fires in 2017, and believe space weapons were used to create this type of damage. According to this conspiracy theory, Directed Energy Weapons (DEW) were used to deliberately cause the wildfires that ravaged certain neighborhoods in California in 2017. These neighborhoods were targeted because they were located in environmentally protected zones or smart development 5G zones, which made them valuable for development or other purposes. Proponents of this theory argue that the fires were too intense and burned at temperatures that were higher than what is typically seen in natural wildfires. They also point to unusual burn patterns and the fact that some buildings were completely destroyed while others nearby remained untouched. Some people have even claimed to have seen strange lights in the sky or heard unusual sounds around the time the fires started.

An aerial view of the homes burnt to the ground by the wildfires in Santa Rosa, California seem to show buildings that are 100% destroyed by fire next to living, green trees.

Maybe direct energy weapons have always been around. Maybe these weapons were used during historic fires like the Boston fire to destroy unneeded sections of ancient cities.

An aerial view of the homes burnt to the ground by the fires in Santa Rosa, California with a few trees left standing. [56]

Was the Civil War A Demolition Campaign?

Do Photographs during the Civil War Period Show the Aftermath of Cannon Balls and Fire, or Controlled Demolitions?

Did the Civil War even happen? Mud Flood theorists say the official narrative of the Civil War does not seem to match the photographic evidence from the 1860s. The photographic evidence seems to show a series of controlled demolitions sloppily staged as a war with cannon balls in front.

Many Youtube videos pick apart photographs of Richmond and Charleston. These videos claim that the damage from the Civil War actually looks like controlled demolitions from the Army Corp of Engineers.

Richmond during the Civil War

Was Richmond's Damage caused by Demolition, or Cannon Balls and Fire?

Richmond, Virginia was the capital of the Confederacy in 1865. Many photos from Richmond show stone and brick buildings allegedly devastated by fire or cannon balls. Yet, wooden trees were left standing untouched. The wreckage that should be inside this building looks as if it were already completely cleaned up. It looks as if a member of the Army Corps of Engineers demolished empty buildings devoid of furniture, clothes, pots, pans, or other personal belongings.

This photograph shows the Richmond White House after the Civil War, and allegedly depicts damage from cannon balls during the war.

However, Mud Flood theorists, like Jon Levi on Youtube, suggest that the damage to the structures in the photograph may have been caused by selectively demolished explosives or directed energy weapons, rather than by cannon balls. The theorists point out black scorch marks on the stone wall that may have only been produced by a weapon using extreme heat, as well as warped fence posts that could have been melted or weakened by an advanced weapon with a lot of heat.

Additionally, why is there such inconsistent placement of rubble in the foreground? Is it possible that rubble was purposefully placed to look as if this location was destroyed by cannon balls? Why is there so much rubble on the sidewalk, and what is this rubble from? Why is there no rubble in the street or in the grassy lawn behind the wall?

The buildings in these photographs, such as the cathedral in the background, seem so beautiful. Yet the president of that day, Abraham Lincoln, grew up in a log cabin. Does the official narrative of our simple, primitive history contrast with the photographs showing advanced architecture in early America?

The wall on the right seems to contain three to four layers of brick. Yet it's been brought down to a pile of rubble, presumably from a fire. Could a fire or a cannon ball bring a wall containing four layers of brick down?

Why are there so many layers to the walls? Why don't we build with three to four brick layers anymore? Did we suffer a reset in which all our construction methods were changed? These are all questions asked by Mud Flood theorists questioning the official narrative of the civil war who try to reconstruct history using their own eyes.

In the photograph above, one can see the remains of the Confederate Capital in Richmond, Virginia. The foreground is filled with scattered rubble, mostly bricks, which are said to have been torn apart by cannon fire.

However, the amount of destruction seen in the photograph raises questions about the plausibility of cannon fire causing such devastation. How much cannon fire would be necessary to cause this much destruction?

There are inconsistencies in the photograph between the messy piles of debris and the cannonballs that are neatly stacked within them. These inconsistencies raise speculation among Mud Flood theorists about the true cause of the destruction.

The debris in this photo stands in direct contrast to subsequent photos in the Richmond photoshoot showing buildings completely cleaned out of debris.

The photograph above displays the ruins of Richmond, with buildings that appear to be sophisticated and durable, featuring stone or brick materials, columns, spires, and bell towers. Despite their sturdy construction, we are told these buildings were burnt down during a time of war.

Notice how the cannonballs displayed in the picture do not seem to fit in the cannons and appear to be deliberately placed for effect. Additionally, the soldier featured in the photo looks undisturbed and peaceful, rather than being alert and prepared for potential attack. The level of destruction raises questions about whether cannonballs were really used to destroy these buildings, or advanced techniques under the guise of war destruction.

Observe how muddy the ground is. Did this land suffer from a mud flood which caused the land to lie barren for a certain period?

The Gallego flour Mills in Richmond, Virginia, located near the James River, were once the largest mills in the south. However, the official narrative is that they were devastated during the Civil War.

According to Mud Flood theorists, the Army Corps of Engineers used advanced weapons to demolish these buildings, or at least employed selective demolition techniques using gunpowder. The brick walls appear to be incredibly thick with multiple layers of brick, and it would take an extremely powerful weapon to penetrate them. Moreover, the buildings seem completely empty inside, as if they were cleared of rubble beforehand. It would be difficult to replicate this kind of damage using cannonballs during a time of war.

In the photograph above, taken in 1865, we see the ruins of Richmond with some unusual features, such as two intact light posts and a tree stump still standing amidst burnt-out buildings. These brick and stone structures appear to have been devastated by gunpowder demolition or advanced weapons rather than cannonballs. One of the soldiers looks as if he's posing for the camera.

It is as if empty, brick buildings were demolished rather than fully occupied buildings. Where are the people's belongings who once occupied these buildings? Where are all the civilians now?

Here are pictures of a destroyed locomotive. The ground looks incredibly muddy. The destroyed buildings have multiple layers of brick. According to the mainstream narrative, this is the aftermath of the Confederate evacuation in which Richmond's business district was accidentally torched by its own citizens! It burned to the ground, and the flames were only extinguished with the aid of the occupying Federal Army. How do you accidentally torch a brick building, and have it look like this afterwards? The brick on the destroyed building looks like it suffered extreme heat. It is interesting how a fire could destroy these bricks when bricks are often used to build chimneys in houses. Thankfully, the tree in the background survived the fire. The ground is incredibly muddy. Do the people look like they are at war, or do they look relaxed, bored, or posing as if they know they are being photographed? If the devastation was enough to make a brick building crumble behind and a train stand lopsided, then why are the trees still standing?

159

The above photo shows a general view of the burned district of Richmond, Virginia. Alexander Gardner captured this April 1865 view from the turret of Pratt's Castle on Gamble's Hill. The buildings seem demolished from a controlled demolition, yet strangely empty. There is almost no debris. As if the belongings in the buildings had been cleaned out, or blown away as dust already. Do these photographs depict a war torn city that was occupied, or a city that was already empty years before, with select buildings demolished by civil engineers using gunpowder or directed energy weapons? Where are the personal belongings? All that is left are the most solid materials! Everything has been wiped out. Perhaps the devastation from a disastrous event occurred more than fifty years before this photo!

A destroyed arsenal in Richmond, Virginia after the Civil War.

It seems like cannon balls are everywhere in the foreground, but not in the actual building that was destroyed by cannon balls.

Some historians note that graduates of West Point were allegedly responsible for fighting the Civil War, and constructing much of our infrastructure. West Point had an advanced engineering school. Maybe these West Point grads working for the Army Corp of Engineers were trained in controlled demolition techniques to take out unnecessary sections of ancient cities for the Reset. Perhaps they had access to high tech weapons that have always been here. Maybe there is nothing new under the sun, and all the advanced technologies like HAARP weapons that we have today were possessed by the Elite in the past.

Charleston in the Civil War

Was Charleston a Beautiful, Old City in Ruins at the Time of these Civil War Photographs?

Here is a Boy seated on ruins of Charleston, South Carolina after the Civil War. Many people are shocked to see how beautiful the structures in cities like Charleston were. They seem to come from a culture much richer than they imagined after reading our standard history books.

The photograph above depicts the Orphan Asylum in Charleston in 1864, which was later used as a hospital for the wounded in 1865. This building looks as if it were once beautiful, but appears to be in ruins, with broken windows and a worn appearance. Its condition suggests that it could be older than a century. Perhaps America had elegant and refined buildings that date back to before the Revolutionary War.

The above picture is of Charleston South Carolina, with a view from the roof of the orphan asylum. The city appears fully developed by 1865, with excellent urban planning and a well-organized layout. It raises questions about the traditional narrative of America being a new country where presidents were raised in primitive log cabins during that time period. Does this look like a new city, or a much older one?

These are ruins of the Cathedral of St. John in 1865. This building was destroyed by fire in 1861. What kind of fire would destroy a building with three layers of brick? Ovens, chimneys, and fireplaces are made of brick. Even if a fire were to burn down all the wood in these structures, it seems impossible to burn the brick and scatter it all over the ground. The question is, what kind of force could destroy these structures in this way?

The photograph above depicts children seated near the pillars of the Circular Congregational Church, a well-known landmark in Charleston, South Carolina. The church was founded in 1681 and remains one of the oldest continuously worshipping congregations in the southern United States.

Mud Flood theorists draw attention to the size of the building, which appears to have been constructed for people of larger stature. They also note the numerous layers of building materials in the church's ruins, suggesting that the structure may have been used by multiple generations who covered the church with different facades. This raises the question of whether America was truly a new country in the 1860s or if it was much older, with these buildings standing for centuries.

While mainstream historians acknowledge that the church was indeed founded in 1681, historical revisionists question how such a massive structure could have been built by settlers who had just arrived in America. They wonder whether these Americans were too poor to construct such a magnificent building.

Atlanta in the Civil War

Did Sherman Really Burn Atlanta to the Ground?

It is sometimes laughable to compare the narrative and illustrations from Civil War books with the actual photographs of the Civil War. For instance, most Georgia history students are taught that Sherman burned Atlanta to the ground, and burned all of Georgia via March to the Sea. Some myths were that he stopped in Savannah because his girlfriend was from there, while mainstream historians said the Union captured Savannah to re-supply its troops. Here is an illustration of the burning of Atlanta.

57

Contrast the illustrations showing Atlanta being obliterated with the actual photographs of Atlanta in the Civil War. The few photographs that exist seem to depict the destruction of small portions of railroads. The photograph conveys a sense of stillness and abandonment with advanced, undamaged buildings visible in the background, while a single scene of destruction is depicted in the foreground.

Atlanta first union train station in ruins 1864
(Does this look burned?)

Sherman's engineers tear up a whole six feet of railroad tracks in Atlanta!! How staged is this photo?

Atlanta Destruction of General Hood's Ordinance Train, ca. 1862

This photograph is often used to depict the extensive destruction that Atlanta suffered during Sherman's burning campaign. However, it is frequently misinterpreted as evidence that Atlanta was completely decimated, with only a few chimneys remaining after the war. In reality, this photo is just one in a series that shows a few sections of Atlanta's railroads being dismantled. The picture above depicts a small train station that was demolished. It is plausible that the photographer took these photos to support the narrative that Atlanta's railroads were destroyed and supply lines cut off. Unfortunately, this picture is often presented as evidence that the city was burned to the ground, using the false assumption that the posts in the photo were formerly chimneys from various buildings.

Atlanta Shell Damaged Ponder House is one of the handful of photos showing Civil War destruction in Atlanta. The Potter House, or Ponder House in Atlanta housed Confederate sharpshooters until Union artillery made a special target of it. So, let me get this straight, according to the mainstream narrative, Sherman supposedly burned down all of Atlanta and most of Georgia, but the only photo we have of a destroyed house is this measly 5x8 hole inside a house? How utterly fascinating.

When Historians examine the evidence, they write funny memorials like this stating: "Contrary to popular myth only forty percent of Atlanta was left in ruins".

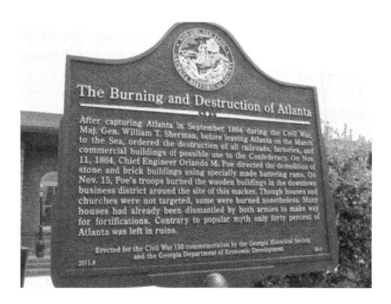

"

The lack of photographic evidence of Atlanta before the Civil War is suspicious. It's almost as if the city was already fully developed like San Francisco, but our "Controllers" decided to create a false narrative that it was burnt to the ground during the war. This would explain why there are no photos contradicting this narrative. It's possible that most of Atlanta's buildings were actually built prior to the war, and the city was not completely destroyed as claimed. This raises the question of whether Atlanta's history has been fabricated to hide the truth about the Reset. Despite being poor after the war, Atlantans managed to rebuild the city rapidly, which makes one wonder if the city was really as devastated as we have been led to believe.

The above photograph depicts Atlanta in 1889. The photograph either shows that the city was built back rapidly after the Civil War, or that the city pre-dated the Civil War and never burnt to the ground. Atlantans allegedly built amazing structures such as the Kimball House, the Equitable Building, and beautiful Victorian Homes rapidly. The First Kimball House Hotel was built in the late 1870s, covering an entire city block at Five Points. With 500 rooms, heating, and an elevator, it was destroyed by fire less than 10 years later.

Kimball House Hotel

The above picture shows the Victorian mansions of Inman Park built after the war . But were these mansions actually built before the Civil War?

Equitable Building – Built 1892, demolished in 1971

Maybe much of Atlanta, such as the Equitable Building, was built before the Civil War, but the elite want people to believe Atlanta was built after. This way, we would not believe the previous civilization was more advanced than our own.

Famous People and their Freemason Assistants

We are taught to hold figures like Abraham Lincoln out as Gods. We were taught to respect these American leaders at an early age. Yet, do we really know who these people were? Why do the soldiers next to him have hidden hands, a common freemason secret societal sign?

President Lincoln at Gettysburg

Posing Bored People

Are they Really at War?

The above photograph was taken in August 1864, and shows Group of Company D, U.S. Engineer Battalion in Petersburg, Virginia.

Are these people worried about war, or are they the "Reset people" cleaning up in an empty, abandoned city in no fear of any violent threat? Have they seen the horrors of war? Or are they well fed with good sleep? Maybe they don't even know they are supposed to act like they are at war. It is strange that civil war photos fail at conveying the hardships of the battlefield.

According to mainstream historians, there are several reasons why Civil War photographs show soldiers lazily posing for the camera instead of photographs of actual combat. Photography was still in its early stages during the Civil War, and the equipment and techniques used were not advanced enough to capture action shots of moving troops or battles. There were also safety concerns, and logistics involved. Logistics: Photographers often had to transport their bulky equipment on horse-drawn wagons or on foot, making it difficult to get close to the front lines.

The Fake and Moving Dead in Civil War Photos

Why did photographers use living people to pose as dead people, or move corpses around?

According to mainstream history, the Battle of Gettysburg was violent and brutal. Union casualties in the battle numbered 23,000, while the Confederates had lost some 28,000 men—more than a third of Lee's army. Yet, photographers never managed to take real photographs of all this violence.

Mathew Brady never photographed dead soldiers at Gettysburg because he didn't get there until all the dead soldiers were buried (or so we are told). Because there were no bodies to be photographed, Brady made a feeble attempt to fool the public by having one of his assistants pose as a corpse in at least three locations. In the example below, Brady's assistant is seen in his phony death pose lying next to the Brian house. In the foreground is the only actual body photographed by Brady, the mummified corpse of a horse probably killed two weeks before.

A Photographer's assistant poses as a dead person for this Civil War photo

More famous snapshots from the Civil War were staged by the photographer Alexander Gardner. Gardner would move corpses To get a better shot.

Corpse poses for his first Civil War photo in Devil's Den

Who moves corpses when trying to document what happened? "False historians! Propagandists! That's who!" Scream mud flood theorists.

Mainstream historians just say that Gardner loved dramatic photos and wanted to make sure Americans saw the reality of war.Two days following the Battle of Gettysburg, Gardner and his assistant Timothy O'Sullivan arrived at the battlefield where many bodies had yet to be buried. The pair spent several days documenting the slaughter. On July 6, Gardner photographed a Confederate soldier in the infamous "Devil's Den." Later, they moved a soldier's body 40 yards over into a spot they thought would have been the perfect place for the sharpshooter to set his sight on the enemy. Why pose a corpse several times if there were thousands of dead people as the mainstream Civil War narrative states?

Corpse walks 40 yards over for his second Civil War shot

Personal Souvenir War Photos

One of thousands of Civil War studio shots. Makes a good souvenir!

When researching Civil War Photography, you may be struck by two things: One, how few Civil War Outdoor-Landscape Photographs there are. And two, how numerous Civil War studio-portraits there are. The above picture is one of many thousands of studio photographs, taken home in pretty gold frames. A mud flood theorist might say that the Reset People were all given Civil War photos to share with their future family to construct a fake history!

Photography during the civil war was allegedly in its infancy, and it required some exposure time. Tintypes were the most common photographic process in the 1860s. The common exposure time was 15 to 30 seconds. It was often taken in a studio. Daguerreotypes were also shot which took 60 to 90 seconds of exposure. Large format cameras common for landscapes would require longer exposure. The photographer was required to fuss with the plates and shroud, and set the camera up for stability. Most landscape photos during that time were taken by professional photographers with giant cameras.

Thus, when you look at the 1860s civil war landscape photographs, you may notice that the photographs were taken by a handful of professional photographers from different angles. The people in the photographs may be in a position to pose for a few seconds. And the photographers generally had a name. Perhaps to become a landscape photographer, you had to be from the 'deep state' and 'in the know'. And take the picture with a deep-state agenda to tell a particular story visually.

Did the Civil War even Happen?

Maybe some of our history is fake. Maybe wars during or after the reset period were faked to have an excuse to destroy ancient cities. The Civil War narrative could also be used to post date buildings that seemed to advanced for the narrative that our ancestors were primitive. Maybe the civil war happened just like historians say, but at a time before reset. And the photographs we see are from a time period after a civil war and reset. Maybe AI was able to rewrite the history books with different dates, using real historical books written at that time as its source.

World's Fairs: Built Up Just to be Torn Down

World's Fairs, also known as International Expositions, were large-scale exhibitions that showcased innovations, advancements, and achievements in various fields such as science, technology, industry, and culture. These events attracted visitors from around the world and were held periodically in different countries.

Many buildings constructed for World's Fairs were allegedly built quickly for temporary use and were subsequently dismantled or destroyed after the fairs ended. We are told that the structures were often made of materials such as wood, plaster, and paper mache, which were not intended to last for long periods of time.

However, Mud Flood theorists believe something is suspicious about World's Fairs. The glorious buildings in the photographs do NOT look temporary! And the technological advancements seemed to come out of nowhere!

The Chicago World's Fair

No way they built all this for the Chicago World's fair in 1893 just to rip it all down!
That's what people obsessed with theories of Tartaria, Mud Flood, Hidden History say.

Nearly half of the United States attended the Chicago World's Fair in 1893. The Fair was also known as the Columbian Exposition in honor of the 400th year after Columbus discovered America. The fair featured 200 amazing white buildings with intricate neoclassical architecture. These buildings were so fantastic, they resembled the United States Capital, the Fountain of Versailles, the London Eye, and the Titanic all rolled into one fair. Yet, they were all ripped down at the end of the Fair!

According to mainstream history books, the buildings for the Chicago's Fair were built merely for temporary use, and were made of a material called "staff". Staff was a mixture made from plaster of Paris and hemp fibers on a wood frame. Because they were temporary, they were demolished after the Fair. This is what we are told.

However proponents of the mud flood believe these buildings were not made of staff, and were burnt down intentionally to get rid of an ancient city. They point out that the structures appear as if they're made of granite blocks, stone, or carved marble similar to other important government buildings around the United States. Their ornate designs were complete with statues of Gods and Goddesses, domes, flowing fountains, columns, porthole windows, spires, delicate carvings, and rounded domes. Temporary buildings are not usually built with such fantastic detail!

Chicago World's Columbian Exposition 1893
Made of Temporary Building Material or Stone?

Staff is a temporary building material that could become a fire hazard if not properly maintained. The World's Fair buildings were mostly torn down because they were made of staff, we are told. However, maybe Staff was only used to build the amusement park section of the Fair. The Chicago World's Fair was designed in two sections: A Refined "White City" with graceful neoclassical buildings that seemed permanent from the photographs, and an amusement park section called Midway with temporary structures made of Staff. The picture below is an example of a building made of Staff. Notice how rough it is and how crude the carvings are compared with the rest of the buildings at the Chicago World's Fair.

58

183

The "City of Light"

When Lighting was in its Infancy

The Chicago World's Fair was apparently wired up for electrical lighting!! This is shocking within the context of history for that time. For the most part, the United States did not have electrical utilities in the 1880s. Thomas Edison did not invent a commercially viable electric lightbulb until 1879. The United States' first utility service began in Manhattan in 1882, and merely served 85 customers with 400 light bulbs living within one square mile. Yet hundreds of thousands of lights lit up the White City in 1893.

Westinghouse was responsible for producing the light bulbs for the display. It won a bid of $399,000 for the fair.[59] Westinghouse manufactured 250,000 two-piece stopper bulbs for the Fair, or 25% of the World's light bulb supply at that time.[60]

Nikola Tesla's new AC generator was responsible for powering the lights. The 1893 Chicago World's Fair was powered by 12 1,000-horsepower AC generators of Tesla's design.

Tesla AC Generator in the Electricity Building at Chicago's World Fair

There are many theories involving the lights and technology displayed at the World's Fair. Some say Nikola Tesla was a fraud who merely displayed ancient technology already held by previous cultures. They say Tesla held 112 patents on privatized technology that was once shared by all ancient people.

Some Mud Flood Theorists also believe that the light bulbs at the Fair could have been wireless. Or the bulbs may have already existed from a previous civilization, but survived the mud flood. However, under Mud Flood theory, these bulbs would have been at least 60 years old. Perhaps the bulbs were newly manufactured, Westinghouse light bulbs. Maybe the purpose of the World's Fairs was to disply the technology that the next culture was allowed to have. Whatever the case, it took someone a lot of effort to manufacture and wire the light bulbs for the Fair.

An exhibition hall at the Chicago World's Fair featured electricity and was filled with electric sewing machines, irons, and laundry machines. An electric kitchen included a small range, hot plate, broiler, kettle, and saucepan.   There was also a moving sidewalk similar to what modern people use in airports. Many Mud Flood theorists point to the pictures of these electrical rooms and claim that this was the last display of ancient technology that we weren't allowed to have. Or maybe this was ancient technology that the elite decided we would have in the next 50 years. Mainstream historians simply say inventors and engineers worked for a long time to put these displays together, and designed the displays to show new technology that was never seen before.

The Electricity Hall at the Chicago World's Fair

Perhaps the society that existed between 1700-1830 already enjoyed the light bulbs, electricity, wireless technology, sewing machines, and stove ranges displayed at the World's Fair.   Or maybe an ancient culture older than the Industrial Age had this technology, and the elite were merely displaying the ancient technology that humans would enjoy during the next period of history. Secret societies might be in possession of ancient technological knowledge from other ages, but only distribute crumbs to society for different periods of time. The Deep State may decide whether a new society gets the flying car, or a wooden plow.

The very first original Ferris Wheel was built for the Chicago World's Fair. This was not just a small ordinary ferris wheel you'll find at a country fair. The original Ferris Wheel held 2,160 people at one time!!! It had 36 gondolas capable of holding 60 people each. It was 264 feet high.

Cultural foods such as cracker jack, juicy fruit gum, quaker oats, shredded wheats and the hamburger were introduced at the Fair.

Were the World's Fairs a Financial Loss?

Mud Flood theorists say "they" could not have possibly paid for all the buildings, inventions, wiring, ferris wheel displays by merely selling cotton candy alone. These Fairs must have been a massive financial loss! Mainstream historians say the Fair had massive financial backing. Chicago's leading capitalists and exposition sponsors financed the Fair. They included Charles T. Yerkes, Marshall Field, Philip Armour, Gustavus Swift, and Cyrus McCormick, who financially backed the Fair. There was also significant financial support from the city and state as well as over $5 million in stock subscriptions from people from every walk of life. Revenues from gate admission, concessions, and exhibitors reached $35 million.[61] Some accounts say there was a profit of $2 million[62] while other sources say the Fair was in debt by $1.5 million.[63] A ticket to the fair cost 50 cents, 25 cents for children under 12, and admission was free for children 6 and under. Perhaps since more than 27 million people attended the Fair, the revenue justified the expense.

If there were a Mud Flood with a cover up afterwards, then the Elite had to get on the same page about the New False Narrative. Maybe that is what the World's Fairs were for!

43% of the United States population somehow attended the Chicago World's Fair! That's pretty amazing for a low tech horse and buggy society!! If a new false narrative was to be sold to future generations, then the elite would have to agree on what that narrative was!! Perhaps over 40% of the US population was ordered to attend the event to receive their military orders. They needed training for their roles in this new society. Did the World need plantation owners? Then what are the new primitive farming techniques? Did the World need teachers? Then what would be taught? Who was going to write the new history books? What old history should be kept? What dates should be fixed? If this Fair was about the Columbian Exhibition, then what story should they invent about Christopher Columbus? Did the World need scientists? Then what science would be allowed?

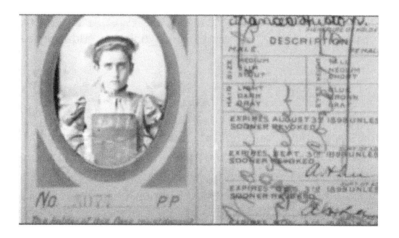

Everything about the World's Fairs seems strange, especially the fact that Passports, like the one pictured above, and Degrees were handed out at the Fair. These degrees were for different careers like farming, priesthood, etc. Personal notebooks were kept in which young adults were taught how to study. Maybe these papers are evidence that people were being trained for their new roles after reset.

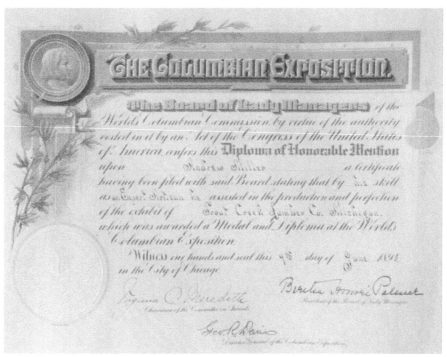

The Above Degree was handed out at the Chicago World's Fair

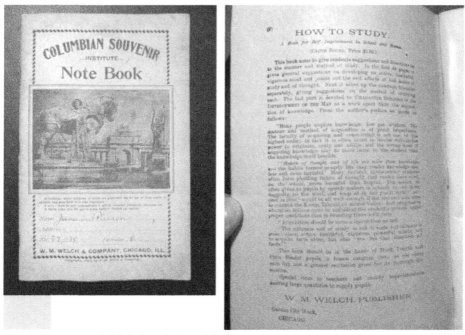

A Notebook taught attendees how to Study.
Why would a Fair teach people how to study?

Demolition of Structures

Allegedly, the Chicago World's Fair only took two years to build, and the structures were temporary. Consequently, most of the buildings and structures were demolished after the fair. Only two structures still stand.

Chicago World's Fair after its Destruction

The St. Louis World's Fair of 1904

The St. Louis World's Fair of 1904, also known as the Louisiana Purchase Exposition also showcased innovative inventions. The fair introduced the electric typewriter, the fax machine, the X-ray machine, and even the ice cream cone to the world. People were on display for cultural exhibits!

This photograph shows a group of Apache Indians, including Geronimo. They are posed in front of tents at the Native American exhibition.

Geronimo was a display at the St. Louis World's Fair! According to Geronimo, he stayed in his place for six months. He obeyed orders from the head of the Indian Department. He sold photographs and signatures for almost two dollars a day and returned home with a lot of money. Was Geronimo a real human being, or a fictional character invented at this World's Fair?

More World's Fairs

While the 1893 World's Columbian Exposition in Chicago is often remembered for its shocking exhibits, other World's Fairs held after 1883 were equally impressive.

For instance, the Great Exhibition of 1851 in London featured the Crystal Palace, a massive cast iron and glass building that was constructed specifically for the event. Although the Crystal Palace was ultimately dismantled and rebuilt in a different location, it remains an important example of Victorian architecture and design.

Similarly, the Paris World's Fair of 1889 was home to the Eiffel Tower, an iconic structure that continues to be one of the most recognizable landmarks in the world. The fair also featured the "Galerie des machines," a massive glass and iron structure that was an engineering marvel at the time. The 1900 Exposition Universelle in Paris was notable for its "Palace of Electricity," which was lit by 40,000 light bulbs and demonstrated the possibilities of electrical power.

The Purpose of World's Fairs

World's fairs were held for several reasons. First, ancient buildings and technology could be dismantled under the narrative that these things were pretend and solely built for temporary use during the Fair. Second, a gathering for the fair could get the elite on the same page about the false narrative they would give to future generations about our history. Perhaps the elite had to decide what ancient technology would be used for the subsequent generations.

Demolition of America's Landmarks

Why were Spectacular Buildings Torn Down Without Good Reason?

Were buildings from a previous civilization called "Tartaria" demolished because they are too beautiful for our modern society?

If the elite are to maintain their false narrative that our ancestors were primitive, then they must destroy buildings indicating how advanced civilization was.

Perhaps a few buildings from the Tartarian civilization were kept to seed our modern society. However, once our modern society became viable on its own, older buildings were phased out.

Many of those believing in a past, advanced civilization show how amazing buildings were torn down shortly after they were allegedly built. The reasons why are mere speculation.

The Chicago Federal Building. "1905"-1965.

The Chicago Federal Building was built in 1905, so we are told. The Federal Building was constructed over a steel frame with exterior walls of brick sheathed with 500,000 sq ft of gray granite from Mount Waldo, Maine. The interior details were accented with terra cotta and scagliola. Doors were oak with brass hardware and "US" molded into door knobs. Mahogany was used in courtrooms and other offices. Marble from Tennessee, Vermont, Maine and Italy was used in corridor floors, wainscoting and stairways.

It was razed in 1965, only 60 years after its completion. The excuse? To make room for a generic skyscraper. It is one of America's Lost Landmarks.

Mud Flood theorists note the excavated mud flood windows typical of historical buildings. Was this a building leftover from the past that was too advanced for modern people?

The Penn Station.   ''1910''-1963

 The Pennsylvania Station in New York City was constructed in 1910, and was built to stand a thousand years, but was sadly demolished only 53 years later through a number of decisions made from a committee of bureaucrats. It was the largest building ever built in America, and the fourth largest of all time. It covered eight acres of land, and was a half a mile long, sitting on two whole city blocks. Architect Charles McKim drew inspiration from Ancient Roman structures.

In 1963, The Penn Station in New York was destroyed because it was "too dirty" and its maintenance cost could no longer be met.

Take a moment to truly appreciate the magnificence of this building - its majestic proportions, the grand columns, and the domed ceiling with each octagonal pattern larger than any individual human. The biggest tragedy isn't that we, in our present age, can't reproduce this building, or even that it was torn down to make way for a sports arena. It's that we couldn't even maintain it.

The Singer Building. ''1908"-1967

In 1908, architect Ernest Flagg completed the Singer Building in Lower Manhattan. So we are told. This gorgeous work of art was a narrow tower with 27 stories. It had a mansard roof and lantern spire.   The photographs speak for themselves. One can observe incredible detailing on its exterior. marble columns, bronze trim. It was once the tallest building in the world at 612 feet.

However, the building was demolished due to lack of office space.

History revisionists say this makes no sense unless the elite are covering up our history. Why would they knock down such a beautiful, famous building which was once the tallest building in the world? Especially considering that it was only built a few decades beforehand? Perhaps this building was just too amazing. And people of this time period would ask whether our past ancestors really lacked advanced technology.

Was this building really built in 1908, or was it leftover from a society that lived before an 1830s reset?

Are Wars Used to Wipe Out Our Past?

Is warfare used as a pretext to wipe away surviving traces of past civilizations? Just like with mysterious fires, World's Fairs, or unexplained demolitions, wars could be used to destroy evidence of our beautiful past.

WWI and WWII

World War I and II struck the heart of Europe, the center of the last advanced civilization. Some of the cities and buildings that were destroyed or severely damaged during World War II include:

1. Warsaw, Poland: The city of Warsaw suffered extensive damage during the war, including the near-total destruction of the historic Old Town. The city was rebuilt after the war, and the Old Town was reconstructed to its pre-war appearance.

2. London, England: London was heavily bombed during the Blitz, a sustained bombing campaign by the German Luftwaffe between 1940 and 1941. Many buildings, like the iconic St. Paul's Cathedral, were damaged or destroyed.

3. Berlin, Germany: Berlin was heavily bombed by Allied forces during the war, resulting in significant damage to many of the city's historic buildings and landmarks, including the Reichstag building or Brandenburg Gate.

4. Rotterdam, Netherlands: Rotterdam was largely destroyed in a bombing raid by the German Luftwaffe in 1940, leading to the loss of many historic buildings and landmarks.

5. Stalingrad, Russia: Stalingrad (now Volgograd) was the site of a brutal battle between German and Soviet forces that resulted in the destruction of much of the city.

6. Dresden, Germany: Dresden was heavily bombed and suffered significant damage during World War II.

These are just a few examples of the many cities and buildings that were damaged or destroyed during World War II, which had a profound impact on the people and societies affected by the conflict.

The Iraq War

Wars in the Middle East targeted certain historical sites for destruction.
The Iraq War, which began in 2003, resulted in significant damage to many parts of Iraq, including its infrastructure, buildings, and cultural heritage. While the war did not lead to the complete destruction of the country, it did result in widespread damage and displacement.

Some of the buildings and structures that were damaged or destroyed during the Iraq War include:

1. Al-Askari Mosque: This important Shia shrine in Samarra was targeted by a bombing in 2006, resulting in significant damage to the mosque and sparking widespread sectarian violence.
2. Presidential Palace: The palace, which served as the headquarters of Saddam Hussein during his regime, was bombed during the war and sustained significant damage.
3. Bridges: Many of Iraq's bridges were destroyed during the war, including the Al-Sarafiya bridge in Baghdad, which was blown up by insurgents in 2007.
4. Power plants and other infrastructure: The war resulted in significant damage to Iraq's infrastructure, including its power plants, oil refineries, and other key facilities.
5. Cultural heritage sites: Iraq is home to many important archaeological sites and historic buildings, many of which were damaged or destroyed during the war. The National Museum of Iraq, for example, was looted in the early days of the war, resulting in the loss of many important artifacts. 15,000 cultural artifacts disappeared in the Iraq Museum.

Overall, the Iraq War had a significant impact on the country and its people, resulting in widespread damage, displacement, and loss of life. The legacy of the war continues to be felt in Iraq and the wider region.

Looted head of a lamassu, cut into several pieces by the plunderers. From Khorsabad, Iraq. Circa 710 BCE. On display at the Iraq Museum [64]

The Syrian Civil War

The Temple of Bel in Palmyra, which was destroyed by ISIL in August 2015 [65]

The Syrian Civil War, which began in 2011, has caused immense architectural and cultural damage to the country. Many of Syria's historical and cultural sites, some of which date back to ancient times, have been destroyed or damaged. The ancient city of Palmyra, a UNESCO World Heritage site, has been severely damaged by ISIS militants who destroyed ancient temples and monuments, and looted and destroyed museums. The Great Mosque of Aleppo, one of the oldest and most significant mosques in the world, was destroyed in 2013 by rebel forces, while other mosques and churches have also been damaged or destroyed.

Numerous cities in Syria, including Homs, Aleppo, and Raqqa, have also suffered severe architectural damage due to airstrikes, shelling, and urban warfare. Many residential buildings, schools, hospitals, and infrastructure have been destroyed, leaving millions of Syrians displaced and without access to basic services. The Old City of Aleppo, another UNESCO World Heritage site, has been particularly hard hit by the conflict, with large parts of its ancient walls, citadel, and souks destroyed.

Ancient Technology

Did People Have Advanced Technology in Previous Ages?

According to Mud Flood Theorists, the past civilization that they call "Tartaria" had free energy. Ancient structures gathered this free energy from the aether, and this ancient tech was dismantled during the reset time.

Churches, cathedrals, mosques, and other buildings of worship could have been aetheric power stations, water stations, and sound resonating acoustical healing centers. The Tartarians allegedly transformed the earth into a circuit board powered by the aether just like the ancients did with the pyramids and temples.

If it looks like something, it must be something!!!! According to Mud Flood Theorists. If a structure looks like a cathode, battery, resonator, or conductor, it could have functioned as such.

Aether

According to some Mud Flood theorists, energy was free and collected from the atmosphere, or aether. Mud Flood theorists seem to use old, alchemical terms for explaining free energy. Is this how a previous generation understood natural phenomena like chemistry and electricity?

According to ancient and medieval science, aether, also known as the fifth element or quintessence, is the material that fills the region of the universe beyond the terrestrial sphere. The concept of aether was used in several theories to explain several natural phenomena, such as the traveling of light and gravity.

A vacuum is rich in aether. And so is the ionosphere. According to Mud Flood theorists, the ionosphere is a source of electromagnetism and can be tapped for free energy. They claim most ancient architectural structures happened and harnessed free energy from the ionosphere

.

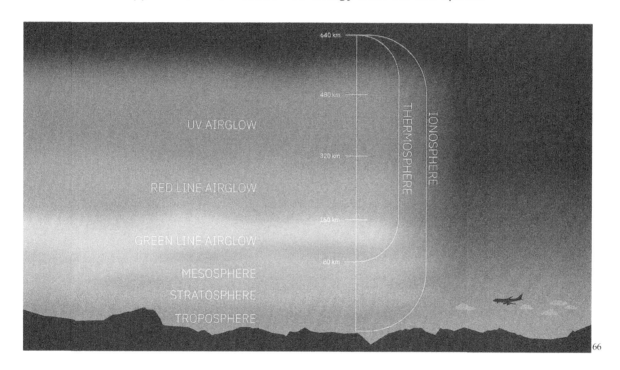

Ancient Alchemy

According to mud flood theorists, people in the past learned alchemy, and used different chemical substances that are now considered rare or hazardous. Their way of understanding these substances were phrased in different spiritual context. Every physical substance was to be understood metaphysically.

Radium

Was Radium Commonly Used Before A Reset?:

History Revisionists claim that old stoves, fireplaces, and bathhouses used radium for heating. Quartz lightbulbs in street lights and house lamps also contained radium and glowed wirelessly. Scientists from our last "Tartarian" civilization placed radium in health and beauty products because it gave health, vitality and long life. Health practitioners added radium to water, because radioactivity was a basic life element. Radium facilitated the process of transmutation - similar to the process of evolution in biology. It could transform one chemical element to another, and thereby held immense power.

Modern chemists and historians say this is nonsense. Radium is highly radioactive and would cause all sorts of mutations, radiation sickness and illness in people playing with it. Radium was only available in small quantities in the past - as in less than a pinch of it. Pierre and Marie Curie had first identified radium as an element in 1898. Marie Curie isolated the first sample of radium in 1910. However, Marie Curie gave herself unpleasant burns improperly handling radium and eventually died from being exposed to radiation. In the 1910s, young women in America who painted glow-in-the-dark watch dials with radium-laced paint became known as the "Radium Girls. Consequently, these workers began dying of cancer and bone disease, and "radium jaw" became a new type of occupational disease. Eben McBurney Byers, an amateur golf champion, was prescribed radium water by his doctor and lost most of his jaw.

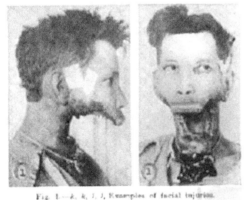

Fig. 1.—A, B, C, D, Examples of facial injuries.

Eben Byers, the Man who drank Radium   Radium in beauty products

Many past writings show how radium could be used in common household appliances or health products. But these writings were based on pure speculation and imagination, according to mainstream historians. Any advertiser who sold a radium-based product was a scam artist. These days, modern chemists chuckle at the scientific lab tests, writeups, books and advertising pamphlets describing radium's potential uses. If you utter the phrase "Radium Suppository" in front of a modern chemist, he will burst out laughing.

Who knows – maybe the establishment is covering up the past's use of radium. Perhaps one could overdose on radium if using it improperly. But if properly handled radium or placed in old-style lead-laced containers, maybe it could prove useful.

Mercury

Was Mercury Commonly Used Before a Reset?

Did alchemists in ancient Tartaria use mercury fused with gold etc to access the ætherial electromagnetic energy and transmit it around the realm? Yes, say answer Mud Flood theorists

Similar to radium, mercury allegedly had all sorts of uses in medicine, appliances, wireless light bulbs, vehicles, and beauty products. Mercury may have switched the AC/DC current in old elevators and lit up the lights in lighthouses perpetually. Mercury allegedly had some sort of ability to transmit aether.

Mud flood theorists believe mercury arc rectifiers were used for charging batteries in old cars. They assert that these older cars ran on direct current rather than the alternate current we have today. Mercury arc rectifiers were used on old London subways such as the mail rail. They say mercury was used for infinite energy and electricity, but this technology is not allowed to be used today.

Mainstream historians say a mercury-arc valve or mercury-vapor rectifier or (UK) mercury-arc rectifier is a type of electrical rectifier used for converting high-voltage or high-current alternating current (AC) into direct current (DC). Invented in 1902 by Peter Cooper Hewitt, mercury-arc rectifiers were used to provide power for industrial motors, electric railways, streetcars, and electric locomotives, as well as for radio transmitters and for high-voltage direct current (HVDC) power transmission. A picture of a mercury arc rectifier is below.

Some say vampires are an allegory for mercury, because mercury can be red, it is repelled by garlic, and red mercury does not make a reflection in the mirror.

Did Antique Fireplaces Operate With Unknown Technology?

According to Mud Flood Theorists, Victorian fireplaces were not designed to burn anything and actually functioned with Tartarian tech. There is usually no room for wood. Or even for coal. The finishes behind the fireplaces were often decorate or shiny. Flammable objects like books were often placed right next to the fireplace. Two pillars were placed in front of the fireplace and had some unknown mechanism to enable the fireplace to heat or cool the house.

Some Mud Flood theorists say these fireplaces heated houses by gathering aether from the atmosphere, or conducting wireless electricity from Tesla towers. They often had metal back plates inside. Many people believed the metal back plate was connected to a rebar, upper tower dome, and outside metal poles within a chimney. These devices channeled the power of aether into this metal back plate, which could either heat or cool the house. Air could be ionized inside the chimney, and the chimney could create a vacuum to either radiate heat or suck out hot air.

Other theorists say the two pillars found in front of these fireplaces contained radium. Radium is a naturally occurring radioactive metal which gives out energy continuously and spontaneously. They believe the knobs on the pillars could be turned to control the heat setting. They believe there was a conspiracy to make nuclear energy seem dangerous to health, and that radium actually sustains health.

Mainstream historians would say all this is silly, and that Victorian fireplaces were designed to burn coal. However, many people point out how the beautiful decorative finishes to these fireplaces would have been ruined if anything was burnt in them. Often, people who own historical houses board these beautiful historic fireplaces up because they could not figure out how they worked.

Were Helium-Powered Airships a Common Form of Transport?

Many Mud Flood theorists think Airships filled with helium were a common form of transport before the reset. They are fascinated with old drawings of air balloons and airships, such as the drawing from the Brockhaus and Efron Encyclopedic Dictionary, 1890-1907. Some theorists like James Horak claim that helium was very prevalent in the last age, and that airships were very safe. After the reset, our Controllers did not want us to use airships or helium on a large-scale basis. The mainstream faked the Hindenburg accident. And the German, Austrian, and Prussian pushed the use of flammable natural gas for airships instead, which limited what Airships could do.

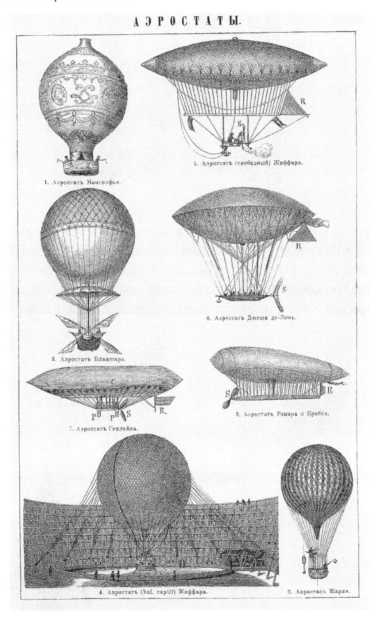

Mainstream historians acknowledge that many past experiments with airships were successful, but claim that these airships were hydrogen powered. Anne-Jean Robert and Nicolas-Louis Robert were two French brothers who built the world's first hydrogen balloon which flew from central Paris on August 27, 1783. They also built the world's first manned hydrogen balloon. On December 1, 1783 Nicolas-Louis accompanied Jacques Charles on a 2-hour, 5-minute flight. Their barometer and thermometer made it the first balloon flight to provide meteorological measurements of the atmosphere above the Earth's surface. In September 1784 the brothers flew 186 km from Paris to Beuvry, the world's first flight of more than 100 km.

The German Zeppelin airship "Hindenburg" was a large German passenger-carrying airship that flew from march 1936 until it had an accident 14 months later on May 6, 1937. It used hydrogen for its fuel rather than helium. In addition to the famous Hindenburg disaster, dozens of hydrogen airships were destroyed by fire, and no American airship has been inflated with hydrogen since the crash of the U.S. Army airship Roma in 1922. The use of hydrogen as a lifting gas for passenger airships was completely abandoned by the late 1930s.

The Hindenburg Explosion

Were Old Street Lights Wireless?

Mud Flood Theorists believe that old street lights somehow harnessed the power of the aether which caused the gasses inside of the upper bulb to ionize and fluoresce. They believe the bulbs were made out of quartz.

Perhaps the bulbs found in streetlights and in homes were not made from glass, but quite possibly from a type of quartz crystal. These bulbs could have contained various substances such as mercury or radium which reacted with the aether. Or maybe the bulbs contained nothing at all and the quartz crystal itself is what reacted with the aether.

Mainstream historians say the lights we see were lit with gas. They claim these street lights were manually lit and had a place to store gas. Cities have distributed gas in pipelines since the 1840s. These gas lights remained in use through the 1880s, and were slowly replaced by electric lamps.

Steampunk Tech

Was Steam a Common Utility hook-up like Gas and Electricity?

Mainstream historians do not argue that steam powered engines were used before the 1830s. . The first commercially successful engine that could transmit continuous power to a machine was developed in 1712 by Thomas Newcomen.   In 1784, William Murdoch, a Scottish inventor, built a small-scale prototype of a steam road locomotive in Birmingham.   The first steamships came into practical usage during the early 1800s; .

However, perhaps steam was used for more mainstream uses in people's homes. And this steam was piped in similar to a gas or electric utility. Maybe steam was commonly used for heating and cooling houses and was used to power personal hand-held gizmos. Perhaps this steam tech was used before historians claim.

New York has a system of steam tunnels that still heat and cool buildings today. There are 105 miles of steam pipes under New York today. Birdstill Holly allegedly invented this steam pipe system in the 1870s. The Holly Steam Combination Company helped roll this technology out in New York in the 1880s. Some of these steam pipes are still operational today. When you walk in New York, you'll often see steam rising from the streets.

Steamy Manhole in New York City [67]

However, is it possible that this was old tech? Were steam tunnels everywhere before the mud flood, and used for basic things like heating and cooling buildings? While there's an official mainstream explanation for who invented these tunnels and when they were built , is it possible that this was the prevalent technology that predated a Mud Flood?

Old fire trucks of the past were basically steam pumps carried on the back of a horse and cart. Allegedly, these steam pumps created steam by burning coal or wood on the back of the cart which provided fuel for the boiler. A vertical water tube boiler provided steam for a pumping engine to force water through the hoses onto a fire. All this machinery was mounted on a horse-drawn, sprung carriage with four, steel-tyred wooden wheels. But were steam pipes everywhere which allowed these fire trucks to be hooked into steam tunnels?

Steampunk is a subgenre of science fiction that incorporates retro futuristic technology and aesthetics inspired by 19th-century industrial steam-powered machinery. Steampunk works are often set in an alternative history of the Victorian era or the American "Wild West", where steam power remains in mainstream use, or in a fantasy world that similarly employs steam power. Is this fictional steampunk genre mixed with the truth of our hidden past?

Was steam and water tech phased out for gas and electric tech? Did we go from a free energy system to a "pay to play" system?

Electric Vehicles are not new technology

Mud Flood theorists say electric vehicles are not new technology. They point to numerous old photographs of electric vehicles. Perhaps these old-style electric vehicles were powered by direct current or mercury arc rectifiers and could not be used after a large scale utility reset.

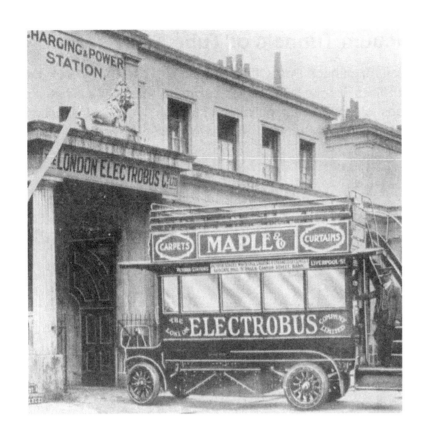

211

Pneumatic Vacuum Tunnels or Tube Tech

Mud Flood theorists love to share pictures of huge Post Offices during the reset. Why were the post offices so large, when today's modern post offices are like little sheds designed to dispatch mail trucks? Perhaps the elite had not decided on how post offices would function, and thought they would function with old tech. And perhaps that tech was old vacuum tube technology, similar to how you give your bank teller a bank deposit.

Post Office, Sydney

Also, mud flood theorists frequently share the story about how a New York subway was built under Broadway using pneumatic technology. Inventor Alfred Ely Beach opened up New York City's first subway line in 1870. It was 300 feet long, and used pneumatic technology. Basically, the subway line was a tube, a car, and a revolving fan.

Why did they Take Our Bells Away?

Mud Flood theorists believe they took our bells away…and wonder why….

Some believe bells functioned as ancient tech. And that most bells were destroyed during reset. The below picture shows bells in Prague. Mainstream historians just say that bells were collected and melted down for ammunition to kill the enemy during war efforts.

Perhaps bells were a very powerful tool of healing. Maybe our previous civilization understood frequency vibrations, and the importance of acoustic resonance. Many believe that bells were destroyed, buried, then replaced, because they emanated a particular vibration which, due to acoustic resonance, had an important effect on human beings.

Ancient Organs and Pianos

Pipe Organ, Brooklyn Tabernacle 1890

According to the Mud Flood theorists, pipe organs healed your organs. They were really the center of ancient cymatic healing centers and energy structures. Healing notes would produce tones, sounds, and vibrations which would heal and energize bodies.

Many urban explorers find pianos in most ancient buildings. Mud flood theorists have many theories as to why there were so many pianos. Perhaps they were used to generate energy somehow. Or again, produce sounds which would heal the body.

Conspiracy Theorists obsess over the fact that the frequency of Standard A was changed to 440. A440, also known as Stuttgart pitch, is the universal pitch used for the musical note of A above middle C, corresponding to an audio frequency of 440 Hz. This pitch is standardized by the International Organization for Standardization. Prior to the adoption of 440 Hz, the French standard of 435 Hz was used by many countries and organizations since the 1860s. However, some individuals glorify the old 435 Hz as the supposed "healing frequency" that was taken away from us. According to this belief, tuning all instruments to a flatter pitch could improve our health and transform pianos and organs into healing machines.

Artesian Wells

More than just Pretty Fountains?

Were Artesian Wells used for generating hydroelectric power, then transmitting it wirelessly?

An artesian well is a well that brings groundwater to the surface without pumping because it is under pressure within a body of rock or sediment known as an aquifer. When trapped water in an aquifer is surrounded by layers of impermeable rock or clay, which apply positive pressure to the water, it is known as an artesian aquifer. If a well were to be sunk into an artesian aquifer, water in the well-pipe would rise to a height corresponding to the point where hydrostatic equilibrium is reached. Were these wells just to draw up drinkable water? To make a pretty fountain? Or was there ancient tech designed to harness the water to generate electricity? Was the top of these towers designed to house a mercury contraption which would transmit electricity wirelessly?

Tower of Grenelle artesian well was drilled in Paris in 1833. Shown here is the Well in 1864.

The Tower of Grenelle pictured above was drilled between 1833 and 1841. The depth of the well is 548 m, and the diameter of the pipe is only 0.17 m. The height of the tower is 43 meters.

Free Energy Within Architecture:

Could Arches have Functioned like Horseshoe Magnets?

Mud Flood theorists claim that the previous society had free electricity, and its architecture helped generate this electricity. Arches could have been instruments of power that harvested, generated, and distributed energy from the aether. Because arches are shaped like horseshoe magnets, Mud Flood theorists believe they functioned like them. These arches are found everywhere in ancient architecture.

68

However, most architectural arches are made of stone, like limestone or granite. Stone does not have much metallic content, it is not usually magnetic, and it is a poor conductor of electricity. Horseshoe magnets are made of nickel, iron and cobalt. Horseshoe magnets are powerful permanent magnets and can be used to generate electricity. An electric current can be created in a loop of wire when it is moved toward or away from a horseshoe magnet. Yet, stone arches are not powerful magnets. If they were, cars wouldn't drive under them or would stick to them. So how a stone arch could somehow be used to generate electricity remains a mystery. Mud Flood theorists may counter this argument by claiming the stone was mixed with quartz, a powerful conductor of electricity.

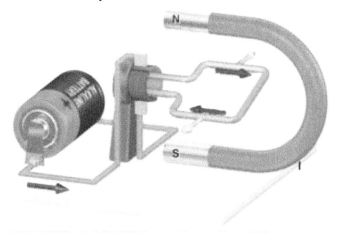

Did Crosses and Spires on Top of Buildings Act as Antennas?

 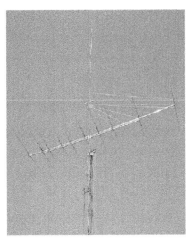

69

70

According to Mud Flood Theorists, the crosses and spires on top of Tartarian buildings were used as aetheric electrical antennas. Crosses on tops of buildings are usually made from copper and gold and are excellent conductors of electricity. But whether they were used to create electricity has yet to be demonstrated.

These antennas could have been connected to a rebar embedded throughout the building's structure.

Did Cathedral Windows Hold Cavity Magnetrons?

Some Mud Flood Theorists believe that Cathedral Windows could have held Cathodes or Cavity Magnetrons. They were never meant to hold glass. Mud Flood fanatics say the word "Cathedral" hints at the original function of holding cathodes. Cathedrals could have been "Cathode-rals'.

A Cathode is a type of negatively charged electrode. The cathode attracts cations or positive charge.

When Mud Flood theorists post pictures comparing the structure of cathedral windows with an electrical device, they use pictures of cavity magnetrons. We are to assume that because Cathedral Windows look like Cavity Magnetrons, they may have functioned as such.

A cavity magnetron is a high-power vacuum tube used in early radar systems and currently in microwave ovens and linear particle accelerators. It generates microwaves using the interaction of a stream of electrons with a magnetic field while moving past a series of cavity resonators, which are small, open cavities in a metal block. Electrons pass by the cavities and cause microwaves to oscillate within, similar to the functioning of a whistle producing a tone when excited by an air stream blown past its opening.

71

Did Baptismals and Gazebos Hold Ancient Engines?

Gazebos and baptismals in old Churches are shaped like octagons. Some mud flood theorists believe that these baptismals and gazebos held ancient engines, and that these engines were dismantled during the reset.

Baptismal Font: Wells Cathedral Saxon baptismal font, dating from about 700 AD[72]

Model of a Soviet Tokamak-10 from 1975[73]

If ancient engines were shaped like today's Tokamaks, gazebos and baptismals could have been ideally housed in these octagonal structures. A tokamak is a machine that confines a plasma using magnetic fields in a donut shape that scientists call a torus. Contemporary tokamaks are used in thermal nuclear fusion power. Modern tokamaks look like they could have fit inside these old structures.

Some octagonal shaped fountains hold interesting structures that look like antennas. Schöner Brunnen ("beautiful fountain") is a 14th-century fountain located on Nuremberg's main market next to the town hall. It is considered one of the main attractions of the city's Historical Mile. Mud flood theorists claim this was an antenna that conveyed ethereal energy to special receivers. These receivers would convert the energy into a luminous plasma to generate light or electricity. Did most gazebos or baptismals before a reset resemble this fountain with machinery inside?

Did Towers and Obelisks Store Electricity Like Batteries?

Mud flood theorists believe that structures such as churches, mosques, castles, or government buildings were actually power generators that would generate electromagnetic energy. This energy was either stored in huge power stations, or in batteries and capacitors, such as towers and obelisks. The assumption is that because a structure is shaped like an electrical device from the outside, then it must have functioned as such. If a tower or obelisk is shaped similar to a battery, it must have functioned like a battery!

In reality, most obelisks are carved from a single piece of stone. Stone is not traditionally used for batteries. Most batteries are made of steel and a mix of zinc, manganese, potassium, and graphite. Batteries use chemistry, in the form of chemical potential, to store energy, just like many other everyday energy sources. Batteries consist of two electrical terminals called the cathode and the anode, separated by a chemical material called an electrolyte. To accept and release energy, a battery is coupled to an external circuit. Electrons move through the circuit, while simultaneously ions move through the electrolyte. Mud flood theorists counter the argument that stone structures would not conduct or store electricity by claiming that the stone was mixed with quartz, a powerful conductor of electricity.

74

Perhaps technology could turn a stone obelisk into a battery. Some researches are trying to turn stone into supercapacitors for energy storage systems, which could create future green smart homes. They are experimenting with an individual micro-supercapacitive stone, such as a hybrid MSC. MSC is made of highly-conductive porous copper electrodes on a substrate, followed by electroplating. [75]

Did Metal Domes Function as Resonators?

Did domes generate specific frequencies for power generation? Mud Flood theorists believe that metal domed buildings, such as the U.S. Capital, could have functioned as domed cavity resonators. They note that these domes often have symmetrical patterning inside that could have helped control resonance.

A resonator is a device or system that exhibits resonance or resonant behavior. That is, it naturally oscillates with greater amplitude at some frequencies, called resonant frequencies, than at other frequencies. The oscillations in a resonator can be either electromagnetic or mechanical and acoustic. Resonators are used to either generate waves of specific frequencies or to select specific frequencies from a signal. Musical instruments use acoustic resonators that produce sound waves of specific tones. Another example is quartz crystals used in electronic devices such as radio transmitters and quartz watches to produce oscillations of very precise frequency.

A cavity resonator is one in which waves exist in a hollow space inside the device. In electronics and radio, microwave cavities consisting of hollow metal boxes are used in microwave transmitters, receivers and test equipment to control frequency, in place of the tuned circuits which are used at lower frequencies.

Dome at Verona [76]

Columns With Internal Iron Rods Could have Functioned as Conductors

Mud Flood theorists believe the colonnades and arches we see everywhere were part of an overall electromagnetic infrastructure which generated free electricity for everyone. They claim that iron rods ran throughout the stone infrastructure, and were complemented with copper and gold roofing. Columns in these structures allegedly would conductor electricity, along with the copper and gold roofing. Mud Flood theorists also claim that the limestone, granite, and dolomite stone in columns was mixed with crystal silicone, or quartz.   And that the quartz had strong electric potential.

Ruins of a Column in Puerta Oscura, showing an Internal Iron Rod [77]

The Temple of Apollo featured enormous columns. Were they somehow wired to conduct electricity?

Could Bricks Conduct Or Store Electricity?

Mud Flood theorists claim a lot of ethereal energy was stored in structures constructed from red bricks and concrete. They claim that red bricks and concrete are excellent conductors of electricity, and operated as huge capacitors or batteries.

79

According to new research, red bricks can be converted into energy storage units that can be charged to hold electricity like a battery and can store energy when required for powering devices. A team from Washington University in St. Louis found that bricks can be adapted and used to store electricity. They found that the iron oxide in bricks can trigger a chemical reaction that enables bricks to store a significant amount of energy. The porous bricks can be coated with a conducting polymer called PEDOT, which is comprised of nanofibers that penetrate the bricks. The brick serves as an ion sponge which can trigger a polymerization reaction .This chemical reaction leaves the pores coated with an electrically conductive plastic, PEDOT. [80]

Mainstream physicists agree that bricks could be useful for storing electricity because of their porousness and red pigment.

Were Red and White Striped Buildings Power Stations?

Mud Flood theorists claim that red and white striped buildings could have been power stations. They say red and white stripes are used to designate power stations today as well as lighthouses. Often, red and white stripes are used on strong magnets, as a way to show they can conduct electricity.

St. Pancras Railway Station [81]

Did bricks really store or conduct electricity? Was the ability to conduct and store electricity inherent in ancient architecture?

Were Lighthouses Power Stations?

Many mud flood theorists believe lighthouses were power stations. Perhaps our previous global civilization harnessed the power of water to generate and transmit electricity. LIke gazebos and baptismals, lighthouses are octagonal in shape. Many lighthouses sport red and white stripes, which would be indicative of a power station. Many look as though they have antennas.

Some mud flood theorists, such as Ewar in his Youtube videos, believe red mercury was used in the cupola of lighthouses. Many cupolas are traditionally painted red, as are many forms of mercury. Mercury rotates and creates a vortex in a current. Mercury may have enabled the lens in the lighthouses to spin and rotate more easily. Mercury might also have been used to help the lighthouses 'antennas transmit signals.
Other mud flood theorists believe lighthouses could have been beacons for AirShips.

Did Previous Civilizations Have Indoor Plumbing?

Mainstream historians claim that running water and indoor plumbing is a modern phenomenon. According to mainstream historians, indoor plumbing started in about the 1840s. In 1940 nearly half of houses lacked hot piped water, a bathtub or shower, or a flush toilet. Over a third of houses didn't have a flush toilet. As late as 1960, over 25% of the houses in 16 states didn't have complete plumbing facilities. So we are told.

But is this true? "No way!", say Mud Flood theorists! People built these amazing buildings, but pooped in bed pans? Princesses living in palaces threw poop out their window into the streets below until plumbing was added in the 1920s. And no one washed their hands either! Rubbish!

82

We have been lied to! Our previous civilization had running water and toilets for the masses like we do. Perhaps the previous civilization fulfilled these functions in slightly different ways.

Theory One: Old WaterWorks Used Disconnected Steam-Tech

Some say the Tartarians used the ancient sewer systems they inherited from other previous civilizations, and also made massive improvements to them. They created a wireless grid, and running water was a major component of this natural electricity system. If Tartarians had pipes, fountains, baths, and tap water, then they must have had toilets!

Perhaps our Controllers confiscated Tartarian toilets and plumbing and disabled their Sewer and Water Treatment plants because they operated on steam-tech. Maybe our controllers switch out our utilities during resets so that humans use different types of fuel sources over time. Switching out fuel sources could preserve the environment of the Earth and serve to promote a false narrative that previous civilizations were less advanced.

Old abandoned Waterworks Systems around the United States are often left out in the open for the public to see. But they may come with false narratives about when they were built. For instance, a historic water in Georgia is the Decatur Waterworks facility. This facility obtained drinking water for the city of Decatur, Georgia, from the local Peachtree Creek and Burnt Fork Creek. We are told that this water works station was completed in 1907 and abandoned since the 1940s. The Decatur Water Works consisted of two aeration and solid removal tanks, two storage tanks, an office building and two dams, one dam on South Peachtree Creek and one on Burnt Fork Creek. This equipment looks like they are hooked into steam-tech which could have since been disabled. Since then, the Waterworks have fallen into disrepair and are covered with graffiti

83

229

Theory Two: Tartarians were Breatharians!

The Mud Flood community has differing opinions on whether or not "Tartarians" who inhabited our previous civilization had bathrooms. Many believe in the "no bathroom" phenomen (i.e., If we don't see bathrooms in Tartarian buildings, they must have been breatharians!) How far you go with this one is your own choice.

Maybe Tartarians held it in! Maybe they shat directly into the aether!

Theory Three: The Previous Civilization Used Cisterns, Chamber Pots, Reservoirs, and Outhouses

Since many 19th century houses have cisterns with pipes and pumps, this type of system may have been available to the average citizen. A cistern is a waterproof receptacle for holding liquids, usually water. Cisterns are often built to catch and store rainwater. These cisterns usually have pipes that lead into 19th century houses with indoor pumps for the kitchen area.

Many Tartarian fanatics like to watch urban explorers like the Proper People on Youtube go into abandoned houses and look around. Many old houses they go into have cisterns, pipes, pumps, and steam tunnels.

Cisterns

San Francisco Plantation House Cistern with Pipe leading to Interior

Cisterns are large containers used for storing water. They can be made from a variety of materials, including concrete, metal, and plastic, and can be located above or below ground. Cisterns were commonly used in the past for collecting and storing rainwater or water from wells, which could then be used for drinking, cooking, and washing. They were particularly important in areas where water sources were scarce or unreliable.

In the 19th century, cisterns were widely used in many parts of the world, particularly in rural areas and smaller towns and cities. They were often made from locally sourced materials such as stone or brick, and were typically located underground to protect the water from contamination and to keep it cool. Cisterns played an important role in ensuring a reliable water supply for households, especially during dry periods or when wells were dry. However, with the development of modern water supply systems in the late 19th and early 20th centuries, cisterns gradually became less common in urban areas, although they continued to be used in some rural areas and in developing countries where access to clean water remains a challenge.

Chamber Pots

Mainstream historians say that those in the 18th century used chamber pots for toilet. People would keep them in their bedroom, or chamber, until you took it out to empty it.

Some Mud Flood theorists speculate that there was a special way that chamber pots could store waste and not stink. Perhaps there were special pieces of furniture that would aid the waste in decomposing and drying out, to turn into good manure. Why would a civilized people waste good manure by flushing it into the water supply?

90 year old Kate Carter in a North Carolina log cabin with her beloved chamber pot, portraying the narrative that people in the past lived primitively.

Antique commodes still exist and can be bought on Ebay. These commodes are nice pieces of wooden furniture with built-in porcelain bowls. Doubters suspect these chairs were built after Reset to support the false narrative that humans had no indoor plumbing.

Perhaps there was a way to vaporize the poop inside the chamber pots. For instance, some vacation homes out in the Alaskan mountains have a lack of water. Water for cooking, drinking, and showering is scarce because it has to be stored in huge containers on the rooftop, and the toilet uses no water. The toilet seals shut and then natural gas ignites and burns up everything in the bowl.

Many say that the commodes would be placed in the hallway of public buildings, and you can find them in old building plans. For instance, royalty at the Palace of Versaille allegedly would poop in the hallways and stink up the building. Other mud flood theorists disagree and say the Palace of Versaille was actually a power station – not a palace. Mud Flood theories seem all over the place. However, many believe the civlization before us was an advanced one and would not poop in buckets!

Outhouses

Did Tartarians use outhouses as their primary source for bathrooms?. Maybe Tartarians thought having bathrooms inside the house were disgusting. However, using outhouses would seem impractical in old buildings such as hotels with 200 rooms.

Are we to believe that the previous population had sewer systems, Fountains, Aqueducts, moats, but no toilets!

Public Bathhouses

Public bathhouses in Rome had latrines. Yet what about other buildings, such as palaces or castles? If one was in a Palace, did they have to run miles down the street to the public bathhouse when the urge hit?

Reservoirs Under Gilded Mansions

According to some mud flood theorists, private reservoirs were commonly used for indoor plumbing in a previous civilization, and they point to guilded mansions as evidence. They believe that many of these guilded mansions were built before the 1834 Reset, and that wealthy individuals kept old houses under the guise of building them during the late 19th to early 20th centuries. These mansions often featured underground tunnels for water pipes, water filters, water reservoirs, and electricity.

One such mansion is Lynnewood Hall, a great surviving Gilded Age mansion in America with 120 rooms. Built for one of the investors of the Titanic, Peter Arrel Browne Widener, Lynnewood Hall features a huge underground water reservoir that was used to service the mansion's fountains and indoor swimming pool. The Proper People, who explored the mansion on Youtube, discovered that this water reservoir also contained a water filter.

The presence of water reservoirs, pipes, filters, and tunnels in these old houses raises the question of why they would not also feature some sort of indoor plumbing. Mud flood theorists believe that private reservoirs were used for this purpose, and that these structures provide evidence of a previous civilization that utilized advanced plumbing systems.

While these stories and theories are fascinating, they do leave many questions unanswered. It is up to individual researchers to examine the evidence and draw their own conclusions about the history of indoor plumbing and water systems in past civilizations.

Star forts

Did Star forts create electricity by channeling water?
Did they have Sound Healing Technology?

Many mud flood theorists claim that star forts used hidden or suppressed technologies to generate electricity. This theory suggests that the distinctive shape of star forts, which were constructed in Europe and other parts of the world in the 16th to 19th centuries, was designed to harness and generate electrical energy or use sound healing technology.

Mainstream historians say star forts are polygonal forts with bastions at the corners that look like stars from above. They were used during the gunpowder era but have origins in medieval fortresses. According to mainstream historians, Star forts were developed in response to new weaponry technology in the late 15th and early 16th centuries, primarily in Italy, and spread throughout Europe. They were heavily employed in fortification building for 150 years until the mid-1700s. Star forts played a critical role in battles and sieges, and their design had a formative influence on the pattern of the renaissance ideal city.

Star forts are fortifications built in the shape of a star with multiple points. They were usually built near cities and were used for defense during wars. The star shape allowed for better coverage and no dead zones, and the forts were often surrounded by water. The passage includes examples of different types of star forts and their complex designs, which were supposedly built quickly for war purposes. The forts were said to deflect cannonballs and had no dead zones for attackers to hide in. . Star forts were found all around the world, and their purpose was not always strictly military as some were also used as towns or citadels.

Mud flood theorists believe that star forts have nothing to do with war, or at least were not all designed for war purposes, despite being categorized as military installations. They were prevalent in old world cities.

While these structures are called different names, they are essentially the same construction. These forts are multi-layered and often connected to water. These structures have impressive symmetry and design. Many of these star cities and the fact that many of them have additional levels underneath.

Many pseudo scientists believe that water when combined with geometry has the power to heal, or the power to affect other dimensions when combined with intention. Star cities channeled water into intricate geometry. Theorists on the Ewar and Autodidatic Channels mention Dr. Emoto's water crystal experiments. Dr. Masaru Emoto's water crystal experiments involved exposing water to different stimuli such as words, music, and emotions, and then freezing the water and analyzing the crystal formations that resulted. He claimed that positive stimuli such as love and gratitude produced beautiful and intricate crystal formations, while negative stimuli such as hate and anger produced deformed and ugly crystals. Perhaps by channeling water into beautiful geometric shapes, love and gratitude result.

Star cities are larger versions of star forts. They are walled cities with an irregular star shape and large buildings, including cathedrals, often located near water. Some people believe star cities were located on ley lines and energy vortexes. Perhaps these cities were not built primarily for defense, as they were often constructed with small cavaliers.

Many of these "star cities," are massive constructions found on every continent, and often form a grid system. Mud flood theorists believe these cities were part of a connected free energy system that was built to help mankind work in harmony with natural earth energies, which is opposite to what we have today.

Mud flood theorists like Autodidact suggest that the construction of star cities does not match up with the timeline of other historical events.

Various locations where these star-shaped cities can be found include China, Europe, and the USA.

Many star forts are built into the ocean or on islands, raising questions about how the builders obtained the necessary materials. It seems like it would have been impractical to go to all that effort to build some of these forts in these locations for defense.

In any case, many questions are raised about the purpose of these structures, and how they were built.

84

The Grid

Were Ancient Cities Designed in a Grid Pattern?

Many Mud Flood theorists analyze cities on Google Satellite and notice that cities are designed like giant grids or circuit boards, leading to various theories about why this pattern exists. Some believe this grid pattern facilitates the transmission of free energy, while others think it allows for monitoring or the use of electronic weapons. Some think this grid pattern is related to keeping the moon in parity with Earth or sacred geometry. Other reasons for this grid-like pattern is unknown, but some speculate that it's related to ancient infrastructure, electricity, or even harnessing human energy.

Many believe that new construction follows the lines of older roads on preexisting patterns.

Some mud flood theorists like Jon Levi point to many Bird's Eye Maps that were created for most US cities in the 19th century. Some of these cities were very new at the time of the making of these maps. Yet, they all seem to be surveyed perfectly with streets laid out according to the topography of the land. Levi remarked in one of his videos how he spent an entire afternoon trying to survey a single plot of land with modern equipment. Is it unbelievable to believe that a primitive society could have perfectly laid out all these streets without this type of surveying equipment or ability to see things from above? Perhaps it is more believable that advanced cities existed in these places before a reset, and our modern civilization inherited portions of these cities with well-designed street layouts.

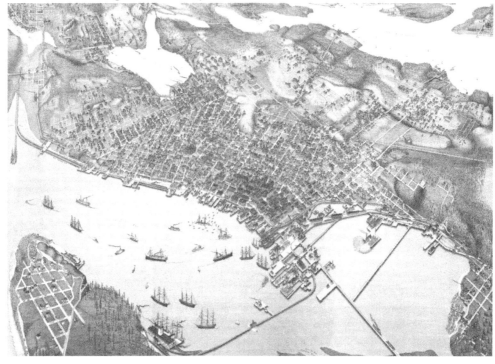

1891 Bird's Eye Map of Seattle

Did Nikola Tesla Know About Ancient Technology?

Mud Flood theorists believe humanity possessed wireless energy before the 1830s. They believe towers, antennas, spires, and engines held in cathedrals, lighthouses, and gazebos all generated and transmitted energy to all things wireless. They believe Tesla Towers were not invented by Nikola Tesla after the 1830s, but were common devices located all over the globe for free energy.

Nikola Tesla was a Serbian-American inventor, electrical engineer, and futurist best known for his contributions to the design of the modern alternating current (AC) electricity supply system.

Tesla's inventions included

- AC Power (alternating current)
- Tesla Coil
- Magnifying Transmitter
- Tesla Turbine
- Shadowgraph
- Radio
- Neon Lamp
- Hydroelectric Power
- Induction Motor
- Radio Controlled Boat

Nikola Tesla's Best-Known Invention was the Alternating Current. When Tesla came to the United States, he worked for Thomas Edison in Manhattan and was promised $50,000 if he could make Edison's direct current method successful. Edison's DC current was not as effective as Tesla's own alternating current. Tesla applied for many patents for his AC power discoveries which were later sold to Westinghouse. AC power has been widely used since its discovery and still has some applications in radio and television transmission.

In 1893 Nikola Tesla demonstrated wireless lighting with luminescent lamps at the World Exhibition held in 1893 in Chicago. In 1894, Nikola Tesla lighted a wireless phosphorus incandescent lamp in a laboratory on Fifth Avenue, and later in a Houston Street laboratory in New York City using "electrodynamic induction," that is by wireless resonance mutual induction.

The Tesla Coil

The most well-known symbol of Tesla's work is the Tesla coil. A tower in Shoreham, New York is the last remaining laboratory with the Tesla Coil. The coils shot electric sparks through the air and circulated the electricity around the coils by alternating current.

Nikola Tesla's Wardenclyffe wireless station pictured above is located in Shoreham, New York, seen in 1904. The 187 foot Wardenclyffe transmitting tower appears to rise from the building but actually stands on the ground behind it. Tesla built the tower from 1901 to 1904 with backing from Wall Street banker J. P. Morgan. The experimental facility was intended to be a transatlantic radiotelegraphy station and wireless power transmitter, but was never completed. So we are told.

In 1896, Tesla was working on oscillations to be used for energy transfer. The idea was to create an oscillator, able to create various frequencies. In 1897 the device was ready, and in 1898, he supposedly was able to oscillate his laboratory in New York. Neighbors called the police and ambulance, fearing that an earthquake was happening. The question is, where is this oscillator now? Conspiracy theorists believe that

Nikola Tesla had several additional amazing inventions that were confiscated by a secret or "deep shadow" government. These inventions supposedly include a death ray, a device for weather control, a free energy generator, functioning a wireless power transmission system, and an antigravity machine. Some conspiracy theorists also claim that Tesla had discovered the secret to unlimited energy and had designed a time machine.

Perhaps structures like the Wardenclyffe Tower prove that humanity had wireless energy before a reset. They believe Nikola Tesla was a figurehead which simply displayed ancient technology that our culture was not allowed to have.

Maybe nothing is new under the sun. Colorful characters like Nikola Tesla could be chosen to show some of the technology we once had, but are not allowed to have anymore after a reset. These remnants of older technologies could be left for those with eyes to see, yet conveniently disregarded by normies as mere fanciful notions dreamed up by a brilliant and imaginative mind.

Were Tesla Towers Everywhere?

Maybe Tesla Towers were everywhere in the ancient world. But we believe these towers were just modern water towers, lookout towers, or radio towers.

The below newspaper says there was an amazing scheme of the Great Inventor to draw millions of volts of electricity through the air from Niagara Falls and then Feed it out to Cities, Factories, and private houses from the tops of the towers WITHOUT WIRES.

Did these Towers actually function as Tesla Towers?

Tower of Jewels, San Francisco 1915 World's Fair

Shukhov Broadcasting Tower. Designed by Vladimir Shukhov. The 520 feet high free-standing steel diagrid structure was built between 1920 and 1922, during the Russian Civil War.

First hyperbolic lattice tower by Shukhov at the exhibition in Nizhny Novgorod 1896

First hyperbolic lattice tower at its present location in Polibino Russia.

Water tower in Kharkkiv Ukraine 1912

Water Tower in Mykolaiv, Ukraine 1907.

Water tower in Kolomna Russia 1902

A Shabolovka Radio Tower 150-meters-high. Completed in 1922

Many Eastern European structures look like Tesla Towers. They are water towers or Shukhov towers, we are told. Shukhov Towers have a hyperbolic steel lattice construction with a diagrid structure. The Towers were used for radio broadcasting.

Our Modern Scarcity Economy:

Could it be that our leaders overthrew Tartaria to usher us into a modern economy based on scarcity? Some suggest that Tartarians had access to free energy sourced from the aether. If this were the case, people wouldn't need to work as much to pay for basic needs like food and rent.

Most wars in modern times are fought over oil, a scarce resource that powers homes, transport, and cooking. If we had free energy, we would have ore freedom and wouldn't have to work as much to pay for it.

Some theorists, like Max Igan, romanticize Tartaria, nothing their architecture and use of copper-lined structures to generate energy from the air. However, it's possible that Tartaria didn't have free energy from the aether but instead used water-based energy or paid for steam and wireless electricity.

It's possible that our controllers reset the utilities after the mud flood, replacing water-based energy with fire-based energy. Perhaps ancient societies enjoyed free energy during a golden age, and we've now entered a "pay-to-play" system as we cycle through dark ages. Did Tartarians experience a golden age or just another dark age preceding ours?

Ancient Infrastructure

Were roads, railroad tracks, subways, and sewers built before an 1830s Reset?

According to Mud Flood Theorists, our infrastructure was already built before America was allegedly "discovered" or "colonized" by Europeans. Podcasters like Max Igan acknowledge that people had to work on the railroads, re-grade some of the cities, and pave the streets. But they believe most of the heavy lifting was already done beforehand. Perhaps the railroads paths were already mapped out and flattened and all the bridges and tunnels for the trains were already built. Perhaps the miles and miles of sewer tunnels in San Francisco were already dug out by a prior culture. Maybe ancient civilizations had subways, and New Yorkers just had to dig out a little mud to get them working again. Did we inherit all this infrastructure from another culture? Let's examine each argument to see if there is any validity to this.

Do Google Satellite Images Prove Cities are Ancient?

Jon Levi posted Youtube videos in which he examined Google Satellite images from places like Egypt or the Great Salt Lake to compare similarities between the land. He noticed lines in the satellite that look like ancient roads. He observed ancient grid-like patterns on land outside Salt Lake City that was supposedly never developed. This grid-like pattern does not seem random. These grid-like patterns that are easily observable on Google Satellite seem like evidence of an ancient civilization's engineering. It seems that when a new neighborhood is built, a landscape designer often chooses to build new roads on top of what seems to be old roads.

Roads are not the only ancient structures that are observable from Google Satellite images. Other ancient structures that show up on Google Satellite that appear to be man-made are
- Sandbars or shaping of land in bodies of water that could serve as ports or gateways for ships. incredible scale to mysterious structures.
- Green circles on land that seem to have fertile soil which could serve as circular farming.
- the presence of unique shapes in remote areas, such as pentagrams.
- Ancient airports that appear to have been constructed in the past, with markings and shapes that are distinct from modern airports. Some airports have been altered over time, but many retain their original shapes and designs.
- Many mud flood theorists like Jon Levi notice structures that look like old railways.
- Old canals.
- Shaping of coastline or waterways for use as Star Forts

Muddy Streets

Were Roads Originally Constructed of Dirt, or Were Old Paved Roads Covered In it?

According to mainstream historians, streets were originally designed to be made of mud or dirt. Muddy streets were relatively easier to use for people with horses and carts compared to automobiles. Horses could navigate the uneven surface and pedestrians could walk without too much difficulty. Dirt roads were the most cost-effective and practical material available. In the early days of settlement, cities and towns did not have the resources to pave their streets with more durable materials like asphalt or concrete. Dirt and mud were abundant and could be easily packed down to create a relatively stable surface. Any ruts or holes could be filled in with additional dirt.

It wasn't until the mid-19th century that cities began to experiment with more durable paving materials like cobblestones, brick, and asphalt. These materials were more expensive but provided a smoother, more durable surface that could accommodate the increasing traffic of horse-drawn carriages and later automobiles.

Mud Flood theorists claim that roads already existed before America was colonized, but that these roads were covered in mud from the mud flood. Most roads had to be repaved, and some had to be re-graded after the reset.

Mud flood theorists also believe muddy streets did not function for society in the 1880s before they were repaved. Jon Levi reposted a youtube video by Whistlin Diesel who demonstrated how wheels on horse-drawn wagons would easily sink into the mud, especially after rain. The idea that people trekked across the country in a horse and wagon seems infeasible and unrealistic without pavement. It also seems impossible for these horse-drawn carts to transport large stones for building purposes in the past to construct buildings such as the Salt Lake Temple. Some of these large stones were incredibly heavy. To think these stones would be transported on a rickety cart with wheels sinking into the mud seems impossible.

Railways

Were Railways Built Before an 1830s reset?

Tartarian theorists claim that all the infrastructure for railways was built before the Earth experienced a reset in the 1830s. They say songs like "I've been working on the railroad" merely refers to laying down a new style of railroad track, not surveying the topography of the land, flattening the land, or building the bridges.

Mainstream historians instead paint a picture of gradual transition from wagonways to railways. The precursor to the railroad was the iron plate-covered wooden tramway in 1805. The iron plate-covered tramway reduced friction and allowed a horse to pull a wagon with more weight.   Wagonways were developed to move coal in the mining areas, and were horse-drawn. Railways were made practical by the introduction of puddled iron after 1800, the rolling mill for making rails, and the development of the high pressure steam engine in 1800. Railways were introduced in the US after 1829. Gradually, private wagonways with iron plates transitioned into public railways with steam locomotives.

A photograph of a Wagonway from 1908

Were Subways Built before an 1830s Reset?:

Mud Flood theorists claim that subways were already there. In their defense, mainstream history is filled with shocking stories of subways that seemed to have been built too fast with future technology. For example, inventor Alfred Ely Beach opened up New York City's first subway line in 1870. Like the deposit tubes at bank drive-through windows, his subway car was propelled by a rush of air from a massive blower. After gaining approval to demonstrate his subway, he built a 300-foot tunnel under Broadway in less than three months. Passengers were able to take a 300 foot ride under Broadway for three years before his train closed.

The bigger question is, was Beach's original subway an ancient technology that we will be able to experience in the future. Why is Elon Musk's hyperloop proposal also based on pneumatic tube technology?

Sewers:

Mud Flood theorists believe that modern people inherited hundreds of miles of sewer tunnels from "Tartarians" after the 1830s reset. This would explain how hundreds of miles of sewers were dug so fast underneath 'new 'cities in the west.

Thousands of Miles of Tunnels Built With Picks and Shovels?

Were sewers built before an 1830s reset? How did workers build thousands of miles of tunnels by hand in just 20 years? According to mainstream historians, workers built hundreds of miles of sewer tunnels under each large American city between 1860-1880 using shovels, brick forms, and manual labor. Boston has 666 miles of underground tunnels constructed in this time period. A small town like Vicksburg, Mississippi has 60 miles. Is that believable? How was this feasible? Did 90% of the population dedicate their time and energy just digging away?

According to mainstream historians, The brick rain drainage tunnels that were constructed in the 1860s were typically built using a combination of manual labor and primitive excavation equipment. In many cases, the tunnels were dug by hand using shovels and picks, and the workers would then reinforce the walls and ceiling of the tunnel with bricks or stone. The tunnels were typically lined with a layer of bricks, which helped to protect them from erosion and collapse. In some cases, the tunnels were constructed using a technique known as tunneling, which involved digging a small hole into the ground and then using this hole as a starting point for the tunnel.

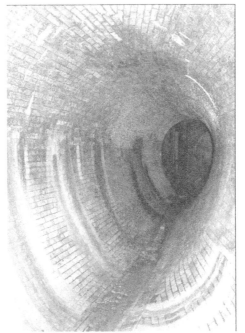

Egg-shaped sewers seem to have been a standard global method of building sewers in the 19th century. How were these perfect-looking sewers done by hand?

Mud Flood theorists believe these tunnels were built before a Reset in 1830. They believe these tunnels were built with ancient tech. Perhaps construction workers used steam operated boring machines and automatic brick-laying machines to accomplish this. They also believe populations were much larger before the reset, and there was more manpower to build the hundreds of miles of sewers necessary for our modern cities.

Here are a few photographs from Boston showing the mainstream narrative of how sewer tunnels were built.

The above photo is from Boston in 1880s. A man is standing in front of workers. Workers are sitting in a low tech wooden form. The form allowed workers to lay bricks by hand within a perfect formation.

The Great Stink: The Sudden Problem of Human Waste

Why did human waste become a big problem in the 19th Century? Was it due to overpopulation, or from disconnecting old water treatment tech?

Many cities started to stink of raw sewage in the late nineteenth century. Mainstream historians claim the stench was new, and was caused by overpopulation.

The Great Stink was a severe environmental problem that occurred in London in the summer of 1858. The city's main water source, the River Thames, had become heavily polluted with raw sewage and industrial waste, which led to a foul smell that permeated the entire city.

The problem was exacerbated by a hot and dry summer that caused the water level in the river to drop, leaving large amounts of sewage and waste exposed to the air. The smell was so bad that it was said to have made people sick, and members of Parliament were forced to flee the Houses of Parliament, which were located along the river, due to the unbearable stench.

The Great Stink brought attention to the need for improved sanitation in London, and it ultimately led to the construction of a new sewer system designed by the engineer Joseph Bazalgette. The city constructed a vast network of sewers, pumping stations, and treatment plants to manage the city's waste. The new system involved the separation of wastewater and sewage, with wastewater being discharged into the Thames and sewage being transported to treatment plants. This helped to greatly reduce pollution in the river and improve public health in the city. Today, London's sewage treatment system is one of the most advanced in the world. London created one of the first separated sewer systems.

Similarly, in the late 19th century, all American and European cities seemed to face the same problem. People allegedly used chamber pots before the 1840s. Sometimes these pots would be emptied into cesspools or rivers. By the 1840s the luxury of indoor plumbing arrived in select households. Toilets were built using this indoor plumbing, and were introduced in the mid 1880s. Plumbing connected these toilets to storm tunnels and flushed it away. These sewers began to reek once the cities became populated. As a result, most of these cities built a combined sewer system which treated waste before combining it with the sewer system.

But why would human waste be a sudden, new problem that 19th Century cities faced? Why didn't ancient systems have a way to dispose of human waste? Every detail of past architecture was thought out in cathedrals, castles, city design, landscaping, stonework and carvings. Yet the ancients never thought about disposing of human waste in a sanitary way? Either humans literally didn't experience bowel movements physically, or we forgot how people in the past disposed of waste. How did people in the 1860s easily lay hundreds of miles of brick lined sewers? Yet, people twenty years later struggled with accommodating human waste later through additional piping and treatment plants?

Were Steam Powered Pumping Stations for Sewers Disconnected in the Reset?

Perhaps civilization had old sewer systems before a reset, but these old systems operated with steam technology. We can see some of this old technology in museums. But we are told that this technology was used in the early 20th century.

The four Austral Otis pumping engines pictured above were contained in the North Engine Room in Melbourne and were all installed between 1911 and 1914 (or so we are told). Each engine was rated at 300 horsepower and was capable of pumping 36 million litres of sewage a day.

Are Sewers Drilled 150 Feet into Bedrock Top Secret?

It is interesting to read social media posts from people who discover tunnels underneath their cities. Especially ones that are 150 deep and drilled into bedrock. From a Facebook Post from Macon, Georgia:

> THIS BLOWS ME AWAY. The tunnels exist on both sides of the river. Some are deep into bedrock below Macon. Some have floors made of Cyprus wood. Some are clean enough to drink spring water. Some are painted white with wood flooring, flowing with clear spring water. And these were dug and constructed in the early 1800s: so it appears. Wow.... the mystery of how and why continues to blow my mind. We are not allowed to know the location or entrances of these tunnels…   JF Fernandez says they go on forever. He told me he has not found the end yet ! JUST MIND BLOWING !!!!!

The larger question is, why are brick lined sewers public knowledge, but sewers drilled in bedrock secret? The answer may be that bedrock lies deeper in soil, at least 150 feet below. And people before the Reset were not supposed to have the technology to drill that deep! Macon, Georgia is in the Piedmont Region of Georgia where sedimentary rock meets bedrock. Macon's sewer tunnels which lay in sedimentary rock only need to be about 20-30 feet underground and are not secret. However, if one walks into the portion of the sewers where the bedrock of Georgia's Piedmont and sedimentary rock of its Coastal Plains meet, they may find the tunnels drilled through bedrock which are about 150 feet deep. If Macon, Georgia has bedrock tunnels, then does Atlanta also secretly have ancient sewers 150 deep under bedrock?

There are no public websites with pictures of Atlanta's old 19th century sewers. Atlanta has 1,800 miles of sewer lines, mostly built in the 19th century. But it's a mystery how these 19th century sewers were built, what they were built of, and how deep they are. Atlanta's libraries and sewer websites carefully leave out this information.

Underground Cities and Tunnels:

We hear about how the elite create tunnels for themselves to hide from such things as nuclear disaster. Were these tunnels already built? If human history is full of Resets, were they used before to take refuge from disasters?

Derinkuyu Underground City in Cappadocia, Turkey. [87]

An enormous underground city that once housed 20,000 people was accidentally discovered by a man after knocking down a wall in his basement. When archaeologists later arrived at the site, they revealed that the city was 18 stories deep and had everything needed for underground life, including schools, chapels, and even stables.

In *Native American Myths & Mysteries* (1991) by **Vincent H. Gaddis,** Gaddis states: [88]

> "Throughout all the Americas there are legends of archaic avenues, racial memories of subterranean passages stretching for miles. After the great cataclysm the ancestral North Indians lived in the vast cavern complex until it was safe to return to the upper world. The story is spread through many tribes, from the kivas of the Pueblos to the lodges of the Blackfeet, from the campfires of the eastern woodland tribes before their dispersion.

> "The Mandans of the northwestern states, some of whom had blue eyes and silky hair … They said the first man to emerge from the tunnels were the Histoppa or the "tattooed ones." Having left safety too soon, they perished. The rest, who remained below, waited until a bright light dispelled the darkness on the surface…"

> "The Apaches' have a legend that their remote ancestors came from a large island in the eastern sea where there were great buildings and ports for ships. The Fire Dragon arose, and their ancestors had to flee to mountains far away to the south. Later they were forced to take refuge in immense and ancient tunnels through which they wandered for years…"
> (Page 39).

PBS posted a Story about the Hopi Origin. According to PBS, Many Native American peoples share a belief that they emerged from the Earth. The Hopi, the westernmost group of Pueblo Indians, is one of these peoples. The Hopi myths claim that Hopis used to live beneath the earth. When it came time to emerge into the world, that Hopi met Maasaw, Caretaker and Creator of the Earth. The Hopi promised Maasaw that they would help take care of the world as a trade-off for staying. After making this promise, Pueblo Indians began a sacred quest, under Maasaw's order, to find "center spaces" and settle. Their populations marked their settlements with spiral insignia. [89]

As we can see, many of these early Americans have legends that they lived underground to hide from disasters in the past. Could our modern secret government underground tunnels, bases, and cities have anything to do with these Native American myths?

We hear about how the elite create tunnels for themselves to hide from such things as nuclear disasters. Were these tunnels already built? If human history is full of Resets, were they used before to take refuge from disasters?

***

It seems that mainstream history paints a picture of reusing old infrastructure in new ways that gradually morph over time. Wagonways give way to railroads. Native American footpaths transform into roads for colonists. Was this gradual progression unbelievable? Were all the tunnels, sewers, and railroads here since antiquity?

Impossible Art

Was all Art Really Done by Hand in the Past?

Was all art done by hand? We are told that art during past centuries was all created with hand tools such as brushes, chisels, files, and knives. However, are some statues, carvings, and relics simply too detailed to have been created without advanced technology?

Amazing Carvings

Was every statue carved with hand tools? We are told that in the 18th century, marble statues were typically carved by skilled artisans using hand tools such as chisels, hammers, and rasps. The process was a labor-intensive one, requiring a great deal of skill and patience. The sculptor would begin by selecting a block of marble of the desired size and quality, and then sketch out the design onto the surface of the marble. Next, they would use a pointed chisel to make a rough outline of the figure or object, gradually refining the shape with other chisels and hammers. Once the basic form was established, the sculptor would use rasps and other small tools to smooth the surface of the marble and add details such as facial features, clothing, or texture. The finished sculpture would then be polished with abrasives such as sandpaper, pumice, or even animal hide to achieve the desired smoothness and shine. The process could take weeks, months, or even years to complete, depending on the complexity and size of the statue.

However, mud flood theorists believe that artists in past centuries had access to tools we do not know about. Perhaps they were able to 3D print statues. Maybe a 3D machine could create a cast, and a liquid marble mixture could be poured into that cast and harden.

Marble Statues

91

Here, a statue depicts an angel is freeing a fisherman by introducing him to the Bible. Over the last 250 years Queirolo's marble netting has been regarded as one of the finest pieces of stonemasonry ever created and 20th-century Italian novelist Matilde Serao described *Il Disinganno* as "a singular closure of life, a singular term for all sublimities, all passions, all loves."

When seeing these works of art, Mud Flood theorists say this was definitely not made with hammer and chisel. Some sort of technology must have been used! Maybe a real rope was dipped in decorative cement. Maybe the statue was somehow 3D printed. Maybe the marble was poured into some sort of cast with a technology we don't understand. Maybe somehow people were petrified! Maybe it was originally clay, and somehow reconstituted into marble. Or, maybe just old fashioned hard work and a highly developed skill set!

Many mud flood theorists are fascinated with the work of Bernini. Bernini carved more than a hundred statues like the one below.

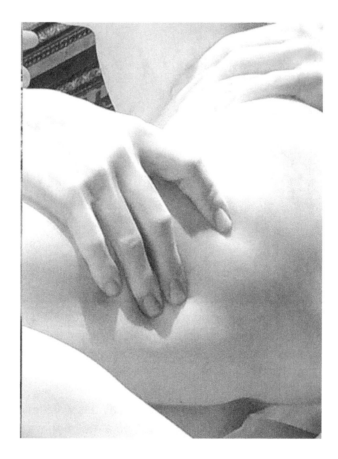

Bernini carved the work "The Kidnapping of Proserpina"when he was 23 years old. There are no skin indentations in the statue.

Art critiques think these carved statues are mind blowing. Mud Flood theorists simply think these statues would be impossible to carve by hand and chisel.

The detail in these Ancient Statues are as if they were 3D printed. The Art of Casting and Sculpting Artificial Stone like Clay is currently known as Geoplolymer. Maybe stonemasons and sculptors shared this as common knowledge in the past.

Veiled Lady, Artist Corradini[93]

Devil's Ball of Ancient China

A puzzle ball on display at the Overseas Museum, Breman

The "Devil's Balls" of ancient Chinese masters were intricate metal or stone sculptures composed of several interlocking spheres. Inside each sphere is an additional 5 to 20 other balls, unconnected and free-moving. Each one is covered with a delicate engraving that never repeats itself. We are told that these masters created them by drilling conical holes in perfect spheres at certain locations, converging exactly in the center; then they marked out future balls with a ruler before cutting them from the center using bent chisels – relying only on their intuition and experience since they couldn't see the surface themselves.

Some say the ancients must have had a way to cast marble, marble, or stone. Maybe they had 3D printers. The intricate and detailed nature of the art from these time periods is truly remarkable and raises questions about how it was created. The intricate patterns and shapes in works such as veils, nets, and interlocking spheres seem almost impossible to have been created by hand alone.

Are Lithographs and Drawings too good to be Done by Hand?

Some historical revisionists believe people before reset took photographs with cameras just like us. During the reset, old photographs were rendered into drawings or paintings instead. Drawings seem too accurate. The artistry is just too good. No artist has the time to paint or draw every detail for unimportant pictures such as ancestry portraits or city drawings. It is easy to take a detailed photograph and make it look like a drawing with an app.

Here are a few examples of past drawings that seem too accurate..

Claude Mellan's 17th Century drawing of Jesus using single line

This engraving from the 17th century is an image of Jesus Christ with a thorn wreath. From a distance it resembles an ordinary drawing, but up close it turns out to be an image created using a single line that spirals out from the center. All the facial details and the transitions of light and shadow are created by thickening this line. The artist is a French man named Claude Mellan. His method of engraving remains a mystery. No one has ever managed to repeat it.

Did Claude Mellan draw this by hand, or use a computer program and printer? Perhaps he simply scanned a photograph of his friend and stuck it in a photoshop program. The printer could change the photograph into a drawing automatically and print it out to look like a drawing using a single line, just like pixels on a computer.

Photoshop in Historical Photographs:

Many Mud Flood theorists show how photographs were photoshopped throughout history. Either for dramatic effect, or to fake a narrative.

Vanilla Skies

The Mind Unveiled Youtube Channel contends that historical photographs were purposefully overexposed to have "vanilla skies". These vanilla skies made photoshop relatively easy and believable. Pale skies allowed an artist to cut out figures and place them on a pale backdrop. Pale skies also enabled a photoshopper to 'fade out' certain portions of a photograph, like the tops of buildings. The below picture is a great example of a vanilla sky used to create a photograph that seemed amazing, yet believable to those without brains! This picture supposedly depicts workers getting rid of a moth found in Elm trees.

Are these photos real and amazing, or fake, impossible, and photoshopped?

Does the above photo depict the Statue of Liberty, or the Statue of Photoshop? According to some, transporting a statue like the Statue of Liberty from Paris to the United States would have been a nearly impossible feat. The patina, or surface oxidation, takes 6 years for copper. If it was reassembled, bare metal would have to be exposed to be able to re-solder and rivet holes never line up, once disassembled and would need to be re-drilled.

On the contrary, photo manipulation only requires a scalpel and steady hand.

The Fake Construction of the Eiffel Tower

Many people say the Eiffel Tower Construction photos look doctored.

Note how the top of the iron bars are faded into an overexposed vanilla sky.

Also notice also how there is an outline cut around each of the workers. This looks like an old-style of photoshop.

Why did they fake the construction of the Eiffel Tower? What is the purpose of photoshopping construction photos? Perhaps these structures were built before an 1830s mud flood event, and our Controllers gave a false narrative that a lot of our structures were built after the reset period.

Today's historians say that the Eiffel Tower was built in Paris, France, and is one of the most recognizable landmarks in the world. Construction began in 1887 and was completed in 1889, just in time for the World's Fair held in Paris that year. It was designed by the French engineer Gustave Eiffel, who also contributed to the construction of the Statue of Liberty. The tower stands at a height of 1,063 feet and was the tallest man-made structure in the world at the time of its completion. The tower was originally intended to be a temporary structure, but its popularity with both locals and tourists ensured its permanent place in the Parisian skyline.

Why would such an enormous structure like the Eiffel Tower be intended for temporary use at a World's Fair? Seems like a lot of effort to sell cotton candy!

Why do Mud Flood Theorists Call our Last Civilization Tartaria?

And Was it Really Germania?

Was Tartaria actually a World Empire that spread amazing architecture all over the earth? Was this Empire wiped out, and its existence covered up?

Discussion about an advanced civilization predating an 1830s Mud Flood reset cannot be had without some loudmouth labeling the whole topic "Tartaria". Why are Mud Flood theorists convinced that Tartaria was somehow the center of the last civilization? Where the heck is Tartaria?

Tartary was a term used in Western European literature for a vast part of Asia bounded by the Caspian Sea, the Ural Mountains, the Pacific Ocean, and the northern borders of China, India and Persia. Mainstream historians say European geographers used the term "Tartaria" during a time when this region was largely unknown. In the present day, the Tartary region covers a region spanning from central Afghanistan to northern Kazakhstan, as well as areas in present Mongolia, China and the Russian Far East in "Chinese Tartary".

According to some Mud Flood Theorists, Great Tartaria was the largest empire before the last reset. The Tartarian empire flourished due to its advanced technology, free energy, and grand architecture. It was the largest country on old world maps because it was a global empire.

Perhaps the name Tartaria comes from the Greek word "Tartarus". Tartarus was a mythological place for lost souls to spend eternity in the underworld. Perhaps this name was chosen due to the Tartarian Empire having been buried and wiped out during the mud flood.

266

The Tartarians (or Tartars) were the indigenous people living in the Tartarian empire. The Tartarians were allegedly tall, averaging some eight to twelve feet in height. They would have been considered giants to our current average height. Some mud flood theorists believe the civilizations before thee Tartarians were even taller, with heights averaged twelve feet, fifty feet, two+ miles, etc...each preceding civilization had an average taller height than the civilizations coming after them and each succeeding civilization had an average shorter height than the civilizations predating them. Statutes are diminishing after each deluge and with each new astrological age we enter.

Tartarian-believers theorize that the French Revolution had something to do with burying the existence of Tartaria. Some believe Napoleon had a Girlfriend who was Russian, and Napoleon used the French Revolution and the French invasion of Russia in 1812 to cover up any evidence that Tartaria was a great empire to please her.

Often Tartarian theorists are skeptical about the mainstream timeline of history in the Medieval ages. They believe that the floods and civilizations of 2,500 years ago actually happened and existed 500 years ago. They cite a man named Flamenco who wrote an alternative version of history. Fomenko believes the mainstream historical timeline was cooked. He claims there were no dark ages, ancient history actually happened more recently, and there was a great Slav-Turk empire centered in Tartaria. Flamenco's theories are explained in the next chapter, under alternative timelines.

Mud Flood Theorists Romanticize Tartaria:

Many Mud Flood theorists romanticize Tartaria. They believe everything created by the Tartarians was beautiful, free, and ideal. They believe we are actually living in the Hell, or in Tartarus, because this beautiful, free technology is hidden from us.

They believe that Tartarians did not have to work so much. Their energy was free, so they did not have to pay for gas, oil, or disposable technology like light bulbs. Or for devices with built-in controlled obsolescence. They believe we have moved from a free society to a "pay to play" society.

Destruction of Tartaria:

Mud flood theorists believe the remnants of Tartaria are constantly targeted for destruction. They believe all wars are fought under false pretenses, just to destroy the ancient ruins of Tartaria. For instance, perhaps during the Iraq war, the artifacts in the Baghdad museum were looted and destroyed. Wars in Yemen and Syria destroyed Aleppo. World War 2 destroyed Dresden, Berlin, and London. Maybe their colonizations were meant to clean up our old history and destroy all the buildings.

Alternate timelines

Most Mud Flood theorists say we are lied to about history. Especially the timeline. Perhaps years were added or subtracted from our history. Maybe the existence of entire empires was buried. Here are some of the prominent theories for Muddies:

Fomenko's Alternate Timeline: No Dark Ages!

Perhaps the Roman and Greek Empire were more Recent! Since nothing happened in the Dark Ages, they didn't occur! Many Mud Flood theorists buy into Anatoly Fomenko's theories. Fomenko wrote an entire series of books concocting theories that question our basic understanding of history. Fomenko's background in mathematics and research on inconsistencies in historical data about lunar cycles led him to conclude that many lunar eclipses and celestial events could not have happened when historians claimed they did.

The New Chronology, as proposed by Fomenko, suggests that historical events that are believed to have occurred thousands of years ago actually took place much more recently. Fomenko claims that the ancient civilizations of Rome, Greece and Egypt actually took place during the Middle Ages, more than a thousand years later than previously thought. According to Fomenko, written history only dates back to AD 800, and events during the dark ages, between AD 800-1000, never occurred due to the lack of information. Most ancient history actually took place in AD 1000-1500, and pre-Renaissance history was made up by writers to please the Catholic Church and reinforce the claims made by the Bible.

Fomenko maps out all of the globe's history and finds that the rise and fall of Kings all around the earth follow a similar mathematical pattern. Consequently, he proposes that perhaps different Kings were actually the same King! Maybe the same story is told multiple times with different names!   For instance, he claims the Temple of Solomon is just Hagia Sofia and Solomon was Sultan Suleiman the Magnificent. Jesus Christ was the Byzantine Emperor Andronikos I Komnenos, who was born in Crimea in 1152 AD and crucified in Constantinople. The existences of Pope Gregory VII, Elisha, Emperor Jingzong, among many others were all inspired by him. The Trojan War was the same thing as the Crusades, which were fought in revenge for the Crucifixion. Ancient Rome actually existed in Egypt and had its capital in Alexandria, Imperial Rome was Constantinople, and Rome in Italy was founded by Aeneas in 1380 AD. Most events in the Old Testament are just interpretations of historical events from the 1300-1400s that have been placed too early
268

by later scholars. Noah is the same as Christopher Columbus, Joan of Arc is Deborah, the Israelite conquest of Canaan is just the Russo-Turkish Horde's conquest of the Middle East.

Many mud flood theorists also expand on Fomenko's idea that 1000 years were added to the timeline. The theory goes that the Roman Numeral J was once written as an I, and people started reading the I as a "1". If a 1 was read in front of every date, then the year 890 would be read as 1890. Perhaps this 1000 year addition helped mask the true timeline of history. The Letter "J" was Invented in 1521. Prior to this, the name "Jesus" was "Iesus" or "Iesous" or "Isa." The Jesuits (Society of Jesus, founded 1540) used the letters "IHS" as an abbreviation for "Iesous." The original King James Bible (1611) used "Iesus." The Quran calls Jesus "Isa." Mainstream historians dismiss his books as complete nonsense.

Fomenko's Theory of a Slav-Turk Empire

Fomenko claimed that a vast Slav Turk empire once existed, called the "Russian Horde". It played a dominant role in Eurasian history before the 17th Century According to Fomenko, the Mongols, formerly known as Tatars or Tartars, did not exist, as such. They did not look like Mongols, but like Russians with European features. They were actually Slavs or Turks. Genghis Khan may have been a Russian, complete with European features. Fomenko claimed that the Mongol invasion was a myth invented by the Romanov Dynasty and the Church.

Many people have been inspired by Fomenko, and created offshoot doctrines of their own. Nikolay Viktorovich Levashov created a system of Slavic neopaganism called Levashovism, in which a great civilization called "Great Tartaria " existed, and where Slavic Aryans were the center of the world in the past.

Mud Flood theorists created their offshoot doctrine from Fomenko concerning Tartaria. If a vast Slav Turk empire existed according to Fomenko, then it must have been the center of the last age before the global mud flood! Mud Flood theorists point to old maps that label a large area of land Tartaria, and conclude that since this land area was big, it must have been an empire ruling the entire earth through the French Revolution.

Mud flood theorists expand Fomenko's reasoning about Tartaria being a great empire, and believe the French Revolution had something to do with burying the existence of Tartaria. .

France was supposed to have invaded Russia in 1812. However, Mud Flood theorists believe this is false, and that France and Russia actually united against Tartaria. Some believe Napoleon had a Girlfriend who was Russian, and Napoleon used the French Revolution and the French invasion of Russia in 1812 to cover up any evidence that Tartaria was a great empire to please her. Many Mud Flood theorists say that there is a clock that exists that shows Napoleon and Alexander on the same clock. The description on the clock says that in unity there is strength. This may indicate that France and Russia were actually allies in the world. And they were fighting someone else - likely Tartaria .

From there, it's a race to see how much history can fall out of your brain and be stomped on the floor below! The whole World must have been at war with Tartaria! Maybe the world was at war with Tartaria around 1600 as well as 1812! For instance, perhaps the battle of Troy was fought at the same time as the overthrow of Genghis Khan. Or at the same time as the Napoleonic war. Maybe all these wars were fought to overthrow the civilization before us, the Tartaria civilization. Maybe Ghenghis Khan was actually at war against the Kzarians. Maybe the Khazarian culture was wiped out in these wars, and they became nomads and wandered around Europe. Maybe the Khazars formulated the war against the Tartarians after becoming

269

nomads! Or maybe the Phoenicians warred against Mongolia. There's a lot of Phoenician architecture implanted over top of Tartarian architecture, like gargoyles. Maybe all the major wars were fought contemporaneously! This type of reasoning can go on endlessly!

Most people feel as if their brains fall out when they argue that the last civilization was centered in "Tartaria". They feel Retardaria. It seems that every mainstream and alternative theory is riddled with deceptions. Maybe the more sane interpretation of all this is that the French empire was the center of the action before a Mud Flood reset. Maybe we can call the French Empire "Germania". Maybe every structure that Mud Flood theorists label as Tartarian is actually Germanian, and the center of the last empire was Germany. Perhaps the French Revolution depopulation and reset process.

When was the Reset?

Mud Flood theorists disagree about when a reset took place. The following are theories you can comb across on the internet.

The Reset Started in 1812.

According to some theorists, the period from 1811 to 1819 was a time of unusual events that they call the Reset. During this time, both America and Europe were at war. The War of 1812 being fought in America. In addition, Indian wars, particularly with Chief Tecumseh, took place.   The French revolution took place at that time. Mud Flood theorists also propose that Napoleon and the French were at war with Tartaria during this time.

The year 1812 was particularly noteworthy in terms of natural phenomena. Large comets, including the Tecumseh or Napoleon Comet with a very low flying path, appeared that year, with the Great Comet of 1811 being the brightest on record. Eclipses were extremely dark at this time.

Significant volcanic activity occurred, with the La Soufrière, St Vincent volcano erupting in 1812 and causing considerable damage and loss of life on the island. The Awu volcano in Indonesia and the Mayon volcano in the Philippines also erupted in 1812 and 1814, respectively.The eruption of the Santorini volcano in Tambora in 1815 was one of the largest and deadliest volcanic eruptions in recorded history, resulting in an estimated 71,000 deaths due to starvation and disease resulting from the eruption's impact on the local agriculture and economy. The ash and aerosols from the eruption spread globally and caused significant changes in weather patterns. In Europe, 1815 was "the year without a summer" due to the eruption of Mount Tambora in Indonesia in 1815, which caused widespread climatic anomalies including a cool summer and crop failures. The effects of the eruption were felt around the world, and the following year was marked by extreme weather conditions, including snow in June and July in the northeastern United States. In addition, there were reports of crop failures in other parts of the world, including China and India. Famines resulted from these crop failures.

The year 1812 was marked by several significant earthquakes, including the New Madrid earthquakes in the central United States. The New Madrid seismic zone is located in the Mississippi Valley and includes parts of Arkansas, Illinois, Indiana, Kentucky, Mississippi, Missouri, and Tennessee. The earthquakes occurred between December 1811 and February 1812 and were some of the largest to ever hit the United States. which were the biggest in American history, causing great chasms to open up in the ground and swallowing whole villages. Mud flows covered large areas.

Vapors and mists known as miasma made people sick. Charles Dickens was a supporter of the miasma theory, which was a popular theory in the 19th century that diseases were caused by bad air or foul smells. Dickens believed that the poor air quality in London contributed to the spread of diseases such as smallpox, cholera, and chimney-sweepers cancer. Dickens often described the foggy and misty atmosphere of London in his writings. In his novel "Bleak House," for example, he famously described London as a "melancholy street of blurred houses and blackened trees" shrouded in a "dense brown fog." His descriptions of the fog in London were so vivid that they helped popularize the term "pea-soup fog" to describe the thick, yellow-brown smog that frequently blanketed the city. There were several disease outbreaks that occurred in 1812 including cholera, yellow fever, smallpox, and typhus.

Lightning was intense, and there were waves of energy that made people nauseous.

The Reset Continued in 1834….

   In November 1833, the Leonid meteor shower occurred which was witnessed across North America. Falling stars filled the sky, with over 72,000 visible per hour according to observers in Boston. Newspapers of the time reported that the meteor shower was so bright that it was possible to read a book by its light alone. The event was so incredible that many people were awakened in the middle of the night by the sound of rocks striking their roofs, as meteorites fell to Earth. In some places, the meteors were so numerous that they were mistaken for a second sun rising in the east.

   Many notable figures, including Abraham Lincoln, Frederick Douglass, and Harriet Tubman, reported seeing it, and it became known as "The Night the Stars Fell." Some interpreted it as a sign of the end times, while astronomers like Denison Olmsted believed it to be a meteor shower. Today, we know that the event was caused by the earth passing through the debris trail of the Tempel-Tuttle comet, which leads to the annual Leonid meteor shower. The 1833 event was particularly spectacular, occurring every 33 years. Was 1833 the time of the Mud Flood Reset?

Maybe Humanity re-lived the period between 1834-1865 Twice!

| French Revolution 1789-1799 | | Mexico wins independence 1821 | | | | | U.S. Civil War 1861-1865 | | | | Reset Generation Live In Tunnels | | Reset Generation Prepares Earth for Our Next Age | |

1780   1790   1800   1810   1820   1830   1840   1850   1860   1870   1880   1812   1830   1840   1850   1860

1st period between 1830-1860   **Reset 1812**   **2nd period between 1830-1860**

Some believers suggest the possibility that humanity may have relived the years 1834-1865 twice, meaning that the Civil War of 1861-1865 occurred just before the Reset event. After the Reset, the calendar was rolled back, and the unusual natural disasters were recorded as if they occurred in 1812, with part of the Civil War recorded as the War of 1812. Then, the calendar was fast-forwarded to 1834, and humanity re-lived the years 1834-1865 a second time.

This theory would explain why photographs of the Civil War look unusual and do not appear to be an actual war, but rather controlled demolitions of old, empty cities. The buildings were empty by the time the "second" 1860 rolled around. The photographs show the Army Corps of Engineers demolishing old buildings that were once owned by a population which was wiped out.

Photograph of Ruins in Richmond, Virginia, 1865.

273

Maybe The Civil War was actually the War of 1812!

Some believers in the Mud Flood theory suggest that the Civil War did not occur between 1860 and 1865, but rather in 1812, which they view as a Reset period. They argue that historical photographs indicate that only a small population inhabited the Earth between 1834 and 1860, and that these individuals may have sought refuge in underground tunnels to shield themselves from nuclear fallout.

Additionally, they speculate that the War of 1812 was mislabeled as the Civil War in order to conceal the lack of activity during the years 1834-1860, and that the perpetuation of this false narrative may have involved book burnings or the removal of legitimate historical texts. In light of modern technological capabilities wherein AI can rewrite long texts in thousands of ways with little effort, it is possible that multiple books about the Civil War could have been created using the factual events of the War of 1812, but with altered dates to fit the revised historical narrative.

If the American Civil War was not actually fought in the 1860s but instead was the War of 1812, wouldn't there be inconsistencies in the dates on the tombstones of fallen soldiers? That would pose a challenge for our controllers, who would have to manage a large number of markers with the wrong dates! Perhaps the authorities falsified the dates on the tombstones to cover up the true history of the conflict. It is worth nothing that during the Civil War, soldiers were initially buried with wooden headboards, often in shallow graves. After the 1870s, the War Department replaced the wooden markers with marble tombstones. Maybe they faked the dates and burnt the books!!!

95

Do Natural Disasters Occur Every 138 Years?

Jason Breshears' website, Archaix, has gained a following among many enthusiasts of the Mud Flood theory. Breshears argues that major catastrophes occur every 138 years on Earth, particularly after four cycles of 138 years, which he refers to as the Phoenix cycle. Additionally, a separate disaster cycle takes place every 792 years. Prior to each disaster, there are reports of objects appearing in the sky, including the Nemesis X object which emerges every 792 years. The Phoenix cycle is also preceded by unusual phenomena, such as red rain, a red moon, and rocks falling from the sky. People mysteriously disappear as well. Breshears has predicted that the year 2040 will be the next reset disaster, coinciding with the Grand Solar Minimum. He believes that we are living in a false reality simulation which he calls a "simulacrum". The real world has created simulations of itself, and the dome we see is not real but a fake projection of what real stars would look like.

His theory that resets occur on a regular schedule linked to astrological events may have some merit. However, adding 138 years to any date that mud flood theorists have used to refer to the past reset would lead to this theory failing.

Christian Theory: The Mud Flood marks the end of the 1,000 Reign of Christ, and Satan is enjoying his short release period.

Many Mud Flood theorists are avid bible readers, and try to relate the Mud Flood to the Chapter of Revelations.

According to Revelation Chapter 20, a "Millennium reign of Christ" will occur in which those who stayed by God's and Jesus's side are "revived". God and Jesus will reign alongside the resurrected for a period of about 1,000 years while Satan was locked away. After the reign ends, the people of the millennium would be taken "blessed and holy" because they were part of the first "resurrection", and Satan would be released for a short period.

According to Revelations, the rest of the dead would not come to life until the thousand years were over.

Some Mud Flood theorists believe that this Millennium reign of Christ has already ended. And that the Mud Flood marked the start of a time of purgatory, or when Satan reigns.

Perhaps the children who were raised in Workhouses, Orphanages, Mental Institutions, Boarding Schools, or Orphan Trains are somehow the cloned dead that were resurrected from tunnels.

Speculation is all over the place on this topic with multiple interpretations, and hours upon hours of podcasts have been produced on this issue.

Could Resets happen between Astrological Ages?

Could Global Resets occur between the astrological ages within the Great Year? Many Mud Flood theorists are fascinated with Prague's astronomical clock attached to the Old Town Hall in Prague. It is the oldest working astronomical clock in the world. It is over 600 years old. It attempts to show the relative positions of the Sun, Moon, and zodiac constellations. Perhaps if we understood how to read this clock, we would accurately predict when our reset periods would be. Maybe each reset happens between astrological ages as depicted on this clock. Does this clock show that we are moving from the Age of Pisces to the Age of Aquarius as astrologers claim?

96

Astrology 101: Astrology is Just a Study of the Life Cycle

Some occultists believe a human spirit cycles through the astrological wheel over many lives. The astrological wheel is often likened to the stages of life. This Circle of Life is as follows:

1. Aries - Infancy: Aries represents the beginning of life, and is associated with new beginnings, self-discovery, and independence. It is ruled by Mars.
2. Taurus - Baby: Taurus represents the stage of being a baby, and is associated with the development of the senses, comfort, and security. It is ruled by Venus.
3. Gemini - Childhood: Gemini represents the stage of childhood, and is associated with learning, curiosity, and communication. It is ruled by Mercury.
4. Cancer - Adolescence: Cancer represents the stage of adolescence, and is associated with emotional growth, nurturing, and family. It is ruled by the Moon.
5. Leo - Teenager: Leo represents the stage of being a teenager, and is associated with creativity, self-expression, and personal power. It is ruled by the Sun.
6. Virgo - Young Adulthood: Virgo represents the stage of being a young adult, and is associated with work, health, and service to others. It is ruled by Mercury.
7. Libra - Partnership: Libra represents the stage of partnership or marriage, and is associated with balance, harmony, and social connection. It is ruled by Venus.
8. Scorpio - Midlife: Scorpio represents the stage of midlife, and is associated with transformation, depth, and sexuality. It is ruled by Pluto.
9. Sagittarius - Retirement: Sagittarius represents the stage of retirement, and is associated with fun, adventure, and optimism.
10. Capricorn - Wisdom and Maturity: Capricorn represents the stage of maturity, and is associated with achievement, status, and responsibility.
11. Aquarius - Second Childhood: Aquarius represents the stage of senility and trying everything once before you die. It is associated with innovation, eccentricity, and humanitarianism.
12. Pisces - Death: Pisces represents the end of life, and is associated with spirituality, transcendence, and release.

According to astrologers, individuals, generations, countries, and even societies all cycle through this wheel.

Astrology 102: The Great Year and the Astrological Ages

Perhaps the timing of Resets has something to do with the Great year. The term Great Year is the period of one complete cycle of the equinoxes around the ecliptic, or about 25,800 years. An ecliptic is a great circle on the celestial sphere. An astrological age is a 12th of a great year, or 2,160 years.

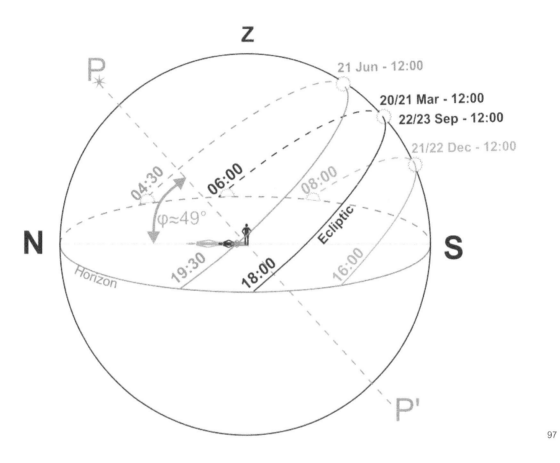

Maybe we experience resets between each astrological age of 2,160 years.

However, if mud flood theorists are correct, we seem to experience resets more often. Could we need to divide 2,160 into 10 to get a number that is closer to the estimated time between resets. Why 10? Many ancient peoples believed that there should have been ten months in a year instead of 12. Julius Caesar added 2 months to the roman calendar. Many occultists believe that a soul descends into matter in 10 stages before reascending. 7 of these stages are manifest, 3 stages are invisible. [98] Many calendars, such as the Chinese calendar, divide time into 12s and 10s. Do we experience resets every 216 years? Maybe we have more frequent resets in the dark ages, and less frequent resets during the golden ages.

Astrology 103: We Are Moving Into the Age of Aquarius

Astrologers believe humanity is moving from the Age of Pisces into the Age of Aquarius.

Astrologers believe that the previous age, the Age of Pisces, began around the time of the birth of Christ and lasted until around the end of the 20th century. They associate Pisces with themes such as spirituality, sacrifice, and compassion, and point to various religious and spiritual movements that arose during this time as evidence of its influence.

Astrologers believe humanity is transitioning into the Age of Aquarius, which is associated with themes such as innovation, technology, and individual freedom. The Age of Aquarius is a time of great change and progress for humanity, where people will come together in new ways and create a more harmonious and just world. The energy of Uranus will inspire people to think and act more collectively. New technologies and innovations would help to solve many of the world's problems. Recent advancements in technology, the rise of social media, and growing interest in holistic and alternative healing practices show evidence of this shift.

Could a Reset like a Mud Flood separate the Age of Pisces from the Age of Aquarius?

Astrology 104: Christianity is a Sun-Worship Religion for the Age of Pisces

Perhaps religions are switched out during resets. Human cultures seem to have religions that are recycled and updated from old ones. Maybe all these religions involve symbolism and allegory based on astrology and the study of the Great Year.

Many astrologers believe that the story of Jesus Christ as depicted in the Bible is not a historical account, but rather a myth based on earlier religious stories and myths. For example, the documentary Zeitgeist: the Movie argues that many elements of the Jesus story, such as the virgin birth, the resurrection, and the 12 apostles, have parallels in other ancient religions and myths, such as the stories of Horus, Mithras, and Krishna. All of these Gods were born of virgins, performed miracles, died or crucified, and rose from the dead. These similarities are not a coincidence. Religions are all based on astrological symbolism for the age they occur.

Jesus is the Son of God, or the Sun of God in astrotheology. It is of no coincidence that Jesus's birth is on December 25. December 25 coincides with the winter solstice, which is the shortest day of the year. After December 25, the days get longer and longer. Because of this, ancients would say the sun was born on December 25.

Jesus is often depicted with a halo in Christian art because he is meant to symbolize an association with the sun. The halo is said to represent the sun's rays, which were often depicted in ancient sun worship as a symbol of divine power and energy.

Similarly, the Virgin Mary's blue cloak represents her association with the night sky and the moon. Blue was considered to be the color of the night, and the moon was often depicted as a feminine symbol of fertility and motherhood in ancient cultures. Therefore, Mary's blue cloak is said to symbolize her role as a mother figure and a symbol of feminine power and fertility. According to many astrotheologists, the Virgin Mary and the Virgin Birth is supposed to symbolize the constellation of Virgo. In some traditions, a sun god's figure was associated with the constellation Virgo, and was believed to be "born" from the womb of the virgin mother. This phenomenon was associated with prominence of the "Three Kings" or the three stars of Orion.

The story of Jesus Christ dying on the cross and being resurrected after three days mirrors the movement of the Sun through the zodiac during the year. In ancient belief systems, if something was not moving, it was "dead". The idea that the sun "dies" and is reborn after three days may have been influenced by the fact that the winter solstice marks the beginning of a three-day period where the Sun appears to stand still in the sky. This period is known as the "solstice point," and it occurs because the Sun's movement through the sky slows down and appears to come to a halt before it begins moving northward again. This three-day period may have been seen as a time of transition and transformation, and may have contributed to the idea of the Sun "dying" and being reborn after three days.

During the spring equinox, the Sun is seen as being "resurrected" and the days begin to get longer. This was seen as a symbol of renewal and rebirth, and was often celebrated with festivals and rituals.

Because Christianity may be a traditional sun-based religion, it is of no surprise that it contains elements of symbolism from the Age of Pisces during this astrological age. The Age of Pisces, which astrologers believe lasted from approximately 1 AD to the present, is symbolized by the fish. The fish symbol was used by early Christians as a secret symbol to identify themselves to other Christians during times of persecution, and it eventually became a widely recognized symbol of Christianity. The bishop's mitre, which is a tall, pointed headpiece worn by bishops in the Catholic Church, is shaped like a fish in order to symbolize the Age of Pisces. Jesus is said to be a fisher of men. the Greek word for "fish" (ichthys) was an acronym for "Jesus Christ, Son of God, Savior" in Greek. This symbolism was deliberately designed by the early Christian leaders in order to create a connection between Christianity and the astrological symbolism of the Age of Pisces.

Many see religion negatively as a tool of social control, used by powerful elites to manipulate and subjugate the masses. Religious institutions have historically been used to justify wars, suppress dissent, and maintain social order, and that they continue to play this role in modern society. Religion can be used as a form of mind control that keeps people obedient and docile, preventing them from questioning the status quo or pursuing their own goals and desires.

However, perhaps religion is the gateway drug to individual study and spiritual enlightenment. Maybe one should not reduce religion as a primitive way to understand astronomy in a dry, existential way.

The Hindu Yugas

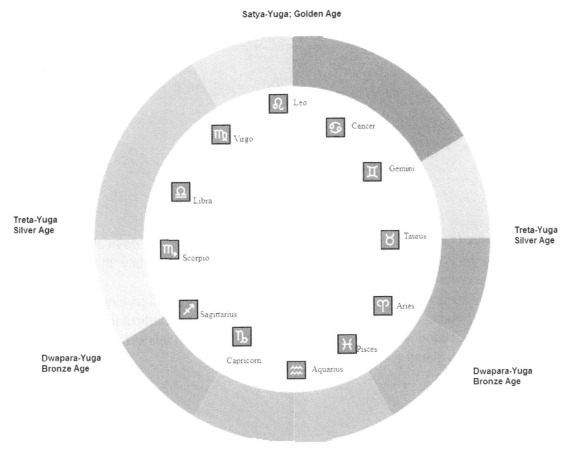

Satya-Yuga; Golden Age

Leo

Cancer

Virgo

Gemini

Libra

Treta-Yuga
Silver Age

Treta-Yuga
Silver Age

Taurus

Scorpio

Sagittarius

Aries

Capricorn

Pisces

Dwapara-Yuga
Bronze Age

Aquarius

Dwapara-Yuga
Bronze Age

Kali-Yuga; Eisen; Dark Age

Hindu philosophy divides humanity's history into four ages: Satya Yuga, Treta Yuga, Dvapara Yuga, and Kali Yuga. Together, these four ages make up the Maha Yuga. The Satya Yuga is the golden age, and lasts the longest. The Kali Yuga is the dark age. Perhaps great resets separate these four ages.

Theosophists and Aryan mystics who subscribe to this philosophy believe that we are currently in the Kali Yuga, a dark age. According to this belief system, humanity experiences cycles of long periods of prosperity followed by shorter periods of darkness. During the golden ages, priests are the rulers and are celebrated, while during the dark ages, slaves rule and society is caste-like. The ruling caste changes depending on the age, and the nature of an age is determined by whether Priests, Warriors, Merchants, or Slaves are in charge. The ideal scenario is when people accept their roles and duties in a world guided by mystical forces. Many people link the cycling ages with astrology and compare the sign of Leo to the golden age because it is ruled by the sun. The illustration above shows how the astrological signs could align with the Hindu Yugas during a great year of 25,800 years. Does the golden age or Satya Yuga relate to the Christian idea of the Millennial Reign of Christ?

Does the Time Between Resets Resemble the Days of the Week?

Is it possible that the generations, such as Baby Boomers, Generation X, Y, and Z, follow a planetary cycle resembling the days of the week? Can we use this planetary cycle to forecast the next reset?

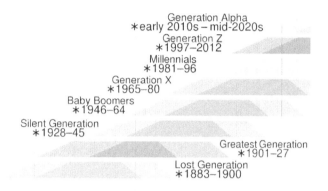

Generation Alpha
*early 2010s – mid-2020s
Generation Z
*1997–2012
Millennials
*1981–96
Generation X
*1965–80
Baby Boomers
*1946–64
Silent Generation
*1928–45
Greatest Generation
*1901–27
Lost Generation
*1883–1900

1880 1890 1900 1910 1920 1930 1940 1950 1960 1970 1980 1990 2000 2010 2020 2030 100

According to the Book of Genesis in the Bible, God created the world in six days and rested on the seventh day, which is where the concept of the seven-day week originates. Ultimately, the question of how long it took God to create the world is a matter of faith and interpretation.

Perhaps we follow this seven-day planetary pattern in short cycles as well as long?

Many occultists believe that each day of the week is associated with a particular planetary body that rules over it. Each planet is associated with certain energies and qualities. In this system, each day of the week is associated with a specific planet as follows:

Sunday = Sun Day
Monday = Moon Day
Tuesday = Mars Day
Wednesday = Mercury Day
Thursday = Jupiter Day
Friday = Venus Day
Saturday = Saturn Day.

An occultist attempting to harness the certain energies and qualities of each planetary day in magical work may choose to perform a ritual for success and power on Sunday, which is associated with the Sun and its energies of vitality and leadership. Or a ritual for love and harmony on Friday, which is associated with Venus and its energies of beauty and attraction.

Since astrology is a study of cycles within cycles, it is plausible that the weekly cycle recurs over 216 years. Predicting the next reset's timing could be achieved through intuitive understanding of the astrological essence of the week, which can be obtained through dedicated ritual practice.

The Missionary Generation may have been influenced by the Sun, due to their honest, upright behavior and relaxed lifestyle. They may have lived during our age's Sunday.

1908, Atlantic City, NJ Beach

According to occultists, Sunday is associated with the Sun and is considered to be a day of power and accomplishment. In Christianity, Sunday is the day for rest and worship. It is a day to practice honesty and morality, and to reflect on these values. The Sun represents vitality, creativity, leadership, and strength. Therefore, Sunday is often associated with these qualities and is seen as a good day for taking action, starting new projects, and asserting oneself.

The Missionary Generation was born from 1860 to 1882, and was the first generation born after a reset. They had the prophet/idealist archetype. The Missionary Generation were idealists and known for their missionary and social crusades, including muckraker journalism, prohibitionism, workers' rights, trade unionism, and women's suffrage. They were led by famous preachers and some were graduates of newly formed black and women's colleges. In midlife, they developed Prohibition, immigration control, and organized vice squads. Vice squads are specialized units within law enforcement agencies that focus on investigating and combating activities related to vice crimes, such as prostitution, gambling, pornography, and illegal drug use. Vice squads 'main objective is to enforce laws related to morality and public order.

Many Mud Flood theorists who observe historical photographs of this generation remark about how rested they seem. It is almost as if they lay around looking bored in photographs. Many of them seem to dress in the same exact outfits that almost came from the same costume box. They are well-dressed, yet sometimes the clothes do not fit them. It is as if the food was already prepared for them, the clothes were already made, and all they had to do is sit around and meditate upon the reset and the future. People find the photograph above odd, as if these people did not know how to dress for an occasion at the beach or pack a lunch.

Perhaps the Lost Generation lived through our Age's Monday. Monday is said to be governed by the Moon. The Lost Generation, or the generational cohort born between 1883 and 1900, may have been ruled by the Moon because their time may have been filled with a false history and a disconnection from their tribe.

According to occultists, the Moon is often associated with illusion, deception, and uncertainty. It can represent a time of confusion or feeling lost, as well as a need to trust one's instincts and intuition rather than relying on external guidance. The moon is associated with femininity, intuition, emotions, and the subconscious mind. It is often seen as a symbol of the hidden or mysterious aspects of life, and its phases are believed to influence the ebb and flow of magical energies. The moon can govern fertility and procreation.

According to mud flood theorists, many of the Lost Generation were orphans riding orphan trains, children working in workhouses or mines, or premature babies displayed in incubator exhibits. They were fed a false history by their teachers, bosses, or parents if they had any.

Wikipedia states that The Lost Generation has a nomad archetype. It is the generation that came of age during World War I. They are referred to as "Lost" or "disoriented, wandering, directionless" in recognition that there was great confusion and aimlessness among the war's survivors in the early post-war years.

The Great Generation may have been ruled by the planet Mars, and lived through our proverbial Tuesday between Resets.

Tuesday is said to be ruled by Mars. In Roman mythology, Mars was the god of war, aggression, and victory. In occultism, the planet Mars is often associated with similar characteristics, as well as with masculine energy, power, and passion. It is seen as a symbol of strength, courage, and action, and is sometimes associated with the element of fire. Mars is often considered to be a planet of assertion, willpower, and aggression, and is associated with the astrological sign of Aries. Careers that are influenced by Mars include Military or law enforcement.

The Great Generation is a term used to describe the generation of people who grew up during the Great Depression and fought in World War II. This generation is also known as the "Greatest Generation" because of their resilience, sacrifices, and contributions to society. They were characterized by a strong sense of duty, honor, and responsibility, as well as a commitment to hard work and self-sacrifice. Many members of this generation experienced poverty and hardship during their youth, which instilled in them a strong work ethic and a sense of frugality.

The influence of Mars is often associated with war, and it is noteworthy that a large number of men from the Great Generation fought in World War II. They demonstrated courage, bravery, and patriotism by serving in the military or supporting the war effort on the home front. After the war, they helped to rebuild and transform American society by pursuing education, starting families, and contributing to economic growth and innovation.

If any generation was governed by Mars or acted as our Society's Tuesday, it would be the Great Generation.

The Silent Generation: Our Age's Wednesday

The Silent Generation may have been ruled by Mercury, acting as our Wednesday between resets.

According to occultists, Mercury is connected with Communication, Intelligence, and Travel. The astrological sign of Virgo is ruled by mercury. Virgo is ruled by the planet Mercury. In astrology, the sign of Virgo is associated with various characteristics, including being analytical and detail-oriented, practical and hardworking, perfectionist, reserved and introspective, and health-conscious. They tend to be very frugal.

The Silent Generation, also known as the Traditionalist Generation, is the Western demographic cohort following the Greatest Generation and preceding the Baby Boomers. The Silent Generation is small in the United States since the Great Depression of the 1930s and World War II in the early-to-mid 1940s caused people to have fewer children. It includes most of those who fought during the Korean War. Upon coming of age in the postwar era, Silents were sometimes characterized as trending towards conformity and traditionalism, as well as comprising the "silent majority".

Like the Astrological Sign Virgo, the Silent Generation is often characterized as being frugal and financially conservative. This generation grew up during the Great Depression and World War II, which instilled in them a strong sense of austerity and practicality. They learned to make do with less, and to save and invest for the future. As a result, many members of the Silent Generation were able to build solid financial foundations and achieve a degree of financial stability and security.

The silent generation was very analytical, as is the astrological sign Virgo. The Silent Generation is often considered to be one of the most highly educated generations in American history. Many members of this generation were able to take advantage of the opportunities that arose in the post-World War II period, including the GI Bill, which provided education and training for returning veterans.

Just as Virgo is the sign of being methodical and detail oriented, the Silent Generation was characterized as being hardworking, methodical, and dedicated to their jobs. This generation grew up during a time of great economic and social upheaval, and they learned to value stability and security above all else.

A Girl Born within the Silent Generation listening to radio in the Great Depression

Boomers may have been governed by Jupiter, the planet of prosperity and lived through the Thursday between Resets.

Occultists believe that the midpoint of a cycle is the peak, much like midday or noon. In paganism, the summer solstice is considered the midpoint of the year. Likewise, Jupiter is to be a planet of prosperity in astrology and occultism.

Did Boomers live through the midpoint of our civilization's cycle, when the times boomed? Was the Baby Boomers 'time of prosperity influenced by the planet Jupiter? Jupiter, the planet associated with prosperity and growth, rules Thursdays in astrology and occultism. This planet has been historically linked to the god of the same name, who was considered to bring good fortune and wealth. The Baby Boomer generation, born between 1946 and 1964, came of age during a time of significant social change, economic growth, increased access to education, and rapid technological advancement. These factors parallel the characteristics of Jupiter. Although the Baby Boomers enjoyed prosperity, they have also been criticized for their impact on the environment, political polarization, and perceived self-centeredness. Therefore, it can be said that Baby Boomers experienced a period of prosperity, possibly influenced by Jupiter's influence.

101

289

Could it be possible that Gen X and Gen Y were influenced by Venus, resembling those living on a proverbial Friday between Resets?

Venus rules Fridays, and is characterized by beauty, love, harmony, balance, creativity, sensuality, and pleasure. Venus is also associated with the arts, music, fashion, aesthetics, romantic and social relationships, as well as luxury, material possessions, and indulgence. Many girls of this generation grew up with Victoria's Secret catalogs, Seventeen and Young Miss magazines, and were encouraged to glamorize their appearance, while men were also obsessed with male beauty when reading muscle magazines. These generations had access to birth control, which led to casual sex in relationships. These generations generally were well to do and enjoyed material possessions such as large housing, lots of clothes, cars, and phones.

Millennials are often seen as valuing experiences over material possessions and prioritizing work-life balance, which aligns with Venus's association with balance. Even though Gen X and Gen Y are tech-savvy, their focus is on social media, online dating, and interacting with friends.

These generations were encouraged to limit family size for concerns about the earth's sustainability, similar to the slowing down of the sun's cycle after the boomers experienced our cycle's noon or peak.

Gen Z: Our Age's Saturday

Perhaps Gen Z acts as though they are influenced by Saturn, and preparing for Bacchanalia on a Saturday night. Perhaps they lived through our Age's Saturday.

Things start wrapping up at the end of a cycle, like a sunset. While midday is associated with fertility, prosperity, and abundance, the end of the day is associated with limiting procreation and austerity. Saturn influences the end of the week. In ancient times, it was considered to be the planet furthest from the sun, and therefore the darkest.

In occultism, Bacchanalia or Saturnalia was a festival in ancient Rome in honor of the god Bacchus, the god of wine, fertility, and ecstasy. It was ruled by Saturn, and came near the end of the year. During the festival, participants would engage in various rituals, including drinking, dancing, and orgies. In ancient Rome, the feast of Saturnalia was held from December 17th to December 23rd in the Julian calendar, and during this festival, a man would be chosen as the "King of the Saturnalia" and appointed to preside over the celebrations. The festival was characterized by role reversals and behavioral license, which included "slaves participating in feasting alongside their masters, masters serving food to their slaves, and the temporary reversal of roles between men and women."

Is Gen Z reminiscent of the festivities of Saturnalia and Bacchanalia, which occurred at the end of the sun's cycle when procreation and abundance were limited? One may argue that Gen Z individuals resemble these festival-goers, as they prioritize online activities over traditional work and social activities. Half of Gen Z identifies as something other than exclusively attracted to the opposite sex, and there are concerns that they may not reproduce as much as previous generations. Perhaps this lack of urgency to start a family is due to a subconscious understanding that life will continue and there will be a reset. Furthermore, Gen Z is experiencing a reversal in the traditional merit-based system, with affirmative action promoting individuals based on their skin color rather than merit. As the last letter of the alphabet, "Z" signifies the end of an era, leading to questions about whether Gen Z will be the last generation to come of age before a reset period, or whether the next generation, alphas, will be the last. Perhaps one MUST use the Zoom app to continue the cycle, as one may need to work remotely to survive urban disasters, such as nuclear war. Does Woke just mean channeling the spirit of Saturn on our proverbial Saturn-day?

102

Generation Alpha is the group succeeding Generation Z, born in the early 2010s and ending in the mid-2020s.

Why is this generation called alpha?

The name "Alpha" comes from the first letter of the Greek alphabet, signifying that they are the first generation to be born entirely in the 21st century.

However, maybe our Controllers chose the name "Alpha" for this generation because they will be the first to live after a Reset! Perhaps a reset will occur when the Alpha Generation comes of age or are in mid-life.

Most members of the alpha generation are the offspring of Millennials. The birth of Generation Alpha coincides with a decline in fertility rates worldwide. Electronic technology, social media, and streaming services have dominated children's entertainment, while traditional television viewership has declined. These changes in technology use have affected how Generation Alpha learns during early development. Studies have found that allergies, obesity, and health issues related to screen time are increasingly common among children in recent years. Perhaps the Alphas who manage to survive their childhood, work, and have a family themselves truly will be 'alpha', as they may resist all the programming and obstacles society has given them.

***

Perhaps secret societies control the traditional political right/left dichotomy along with the influence of astrological forces. Depending on where we are in the cycle, certain goals and objectives may need to be achieved, and society may be pushed in a particular direction.

Those who belong to secret societies may use this knowledge to manipulate the population, steering them in a particular direction depending on the planetary influence at any given time. For instance, if a particular generation is vibrating to the energy of Mars, the planet of war, these elites may use this knowledge to direct us towards certain conflicts or harness our energy in other ways.

Alternatively, secret societies may be tasked with guiding us towards a sustainable future for the planet. This could mean encouraging population growth or advocating for birth control measures, depending on the needs of the planet and the specific planetary influences at play. Ultimately, the extent to which secret societies are using planetary cycles to shape society is open to debate, but it's clear that the two are intimately intertwined.

Old Maps

Mud Flood theorists try to point to a large land area known as Tartaria. Because it was large and marked on a map, many mud flood theorists claim it must have been a great empire. Anyone can go to a mainstream search engine and find old maps of Tartaria.

Tartaria

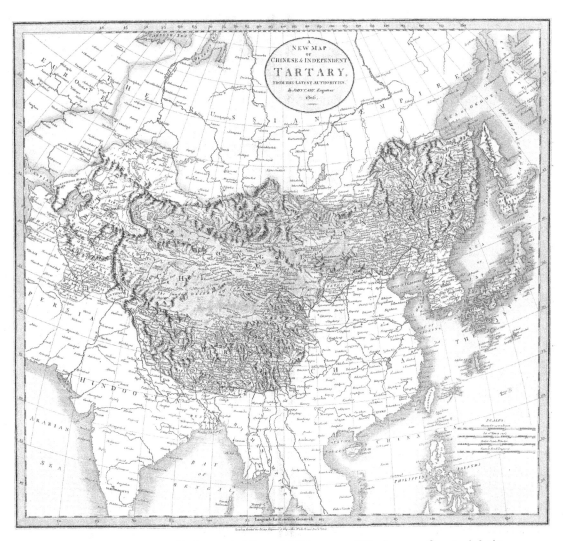

John Carys New Universal Atlas, 1806 map of Tartary or Central Asia

Did Land Masses Disappear after a Natural Disaster?

Mud Flood theorists believe old maps prove that something catastrophic happened in our past.

Perhaps a natural disaster like a mud flood was accompanied by earthquakes, volcanic activity, and changes to different land masses. Old land masses like Frisland, or an island off California, disappeared into the ocean. Maybe different routes of rivers like the Mississippi changed course, and can be compared with old maps.

Is there land up at the north pole?

According to many mud flood theorists, there could be land at the North Pole. They base this theory upon looking at old maps. Especially Mercator's map from 1569, which features a black rock in the center of the North Pole.

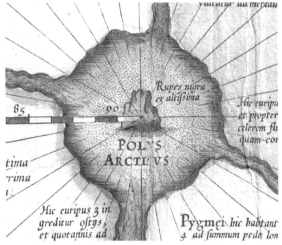

Mercator Map 1569

According to mainstream historians, Mercator was a famous cartographer who lived in the 1500s. He is best known for the "Mercator projection," the method of taking the curved lines of the Earth and transforming them into straight ones that can be used on a flat map. Mercator based many of his maps on explorer travelogs. Even though no one had traveled to the North pole yet, Mercator drew a map of it anyway, based on a questionable travelog written by an unknown source. This travelog called Inventio Fortunata claimed there was a 33 mile wide black rock at the North Pole. Inventio Fortunata also claimed to have found the Isle of Dwarves inhabited by men with long feet. The rivers at the pole ran so fast they didn't freeze.   Mercator drew the Black Rock described in Inventio Fortunata in his map, and labeled it "Rupus Nigra et Altissima.

Many other ancient maps feature four sections at the North Pole.

Did mapmakers in the 1500s simply copy an original map which was false, or did the mapmakers base these maps on actual explorations which took place?

Oronce Fine's World Map, 1531, showing North Pole with four sections of land

North Pole on Mercator Map, 1609

World Map made in 1587 by Urbano Monte, showing four sections of land at North Pole

Admiral Byrd was a well-known American naval officer and explorer who allegedly flew to the North pole in 1926 and 1947. However, this fact is disputed. According to his logs, he said there was land at the north pole, and it was not just water or snow. There were huge areas of land with mountains, forests and vegetation, huge lakes and rivers with animals that resembled mammoths. He is rumored to be a freemason, so not to be trusted.

Mud Flood theorists scoff at Google Earth for using CGI, especially for places around the globe that do not have access to aerial photography. They say Google Earth is not created via satellite, but by airplanes, and that no airplanes fly around places like the North Pole. Therefore, Google Earth just gives us an artistic recreation of remote places, based on the official narrative. Mud flood theorists like Jon Levi and Shelley Sangrey from the "There's no Place Like Home" Youtube channel notice that there's a seam on Google Earth that seems to show us a peak of the "real image" of earth beneath it. This seam seems to portray land around the north pole upon zooming in.

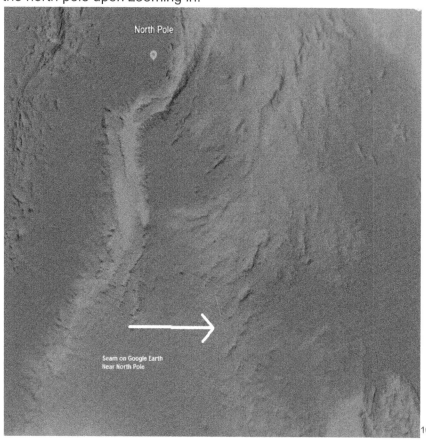

What Happened to Friesland?

Friesland appears to have been born out of the confusion between an imaginary island and the actual southern part of Greenland. Friesland originally may also have been a cartographic approximation of Iceland, but in 1558 the influential Zeno map charted the landmass as an entirely separate island south (or occasionally south-west) of Iceland.

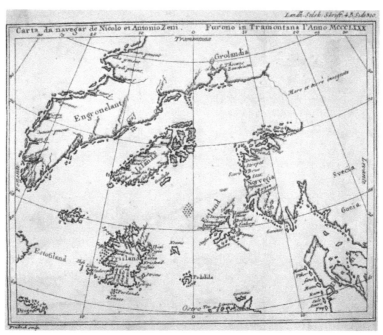

1558 Map of Friesland

What Happened to the Island of California?

California could break off into an island one day! It could sink! It's in an earthquake zone! The kicker? This has already happened!

Many people are surprised to see old maps of America, like the 1636 map below. Or others in the 18th Century. They seem to show California as an Island. This has led many to believe that California was actually once separate from America.

But maybe California sank. When overlaying the maps over modern maps, one will notice that California is actually it's own separate Island and that the water level has actually risen.

Old Illustrated Maps of America With Castles

The definition of Tartaria seems to differ among researchers. Some people refer to Tartaria as an empire centering around a place in Central Asia. Other mud flood theorists refer to Tartaria as a time period in the 1500s-1700s in which people seemed to built stone castles or star forts.

Researchers believe old maps prove that a civilization we could refer to as Tartaria existed in places like America. These old maps often depict a place using illustrations. This is a map drawn in 1546 showing illustrations of large castles in America. Perhaps these maps prove that America wasn't just wilderness with Indians living in teepees in the 1500s, but looked more like medieval Europe. Perhaps Tartaria is from a much more recent time and was left out from the history books specifically because it was hijacked, leading to fake mainstream history and false timelines.

Some of the buildings torn down at World's Fairs in the early 1900s resemble the castles found on old maps from American in the 1500s. Were these buildings really 19th century buildings, or were some of these buildings from the 1500s?

Administration building for California 1894 Midwinter International Exhibition

Genetically Engineered Humans?

Is it possible that our species is re-engineered repeatedly over a series of resets? Perhaps we have portions of our brain and DNA that were switched off by another species that 'owns' us. Maybe humans are a species which is periodically genetically tweaked. DNA leftover from past resets could be switched off and labeled "junk DNA". Many Mud Flood theorists believe that humans were somehow different before the reset. Many believe there were giants! And we were genetically engineered to be shorter.

Giants in our Recent Past

Are we a smaller version of humans or gods from the past? Internet theories claim that Tartarians were tall people, averaging eight to twelve feet in height. They would be considered giants to our current average height of only around six feet.

Some believe that each preceding civilization had an average taller height than the civilizations coming after them. The civilizations before Tartaria could have averaged twelve feet, fifty feet, two+ miles, etc. Maybe statures diminish after each deluge and with each new astrological age we enter. Civilizations in the current astrological age (the Age of Pisces) are shorter in height than civilizations that existed in the previous astrological age (the Age of Aries) and will be taller.

Many people believe that evidence proving that giants inhabited the earth in recent history was covered up. Especially by institutions such as the Smithsonian.

In Lake Delavan, Winsconsin, many believe that there was a lost race of giants found in burial mounds that were covered up. A dig site overseen by Beloit College was excavated at Lake Delavan between 1911-1912, and included more than 200 effigy mounds. 18 skeletons and/or mummies with enormous size and elongated skulls were found.

Picture from lake Geneva Herald Depicting a Giant Discovered in Indian Mounds

The Patagonian giants were a race of giant humans rumored to be living in Patagonia and described in early European accounts. They were said to have exceeded at least double normal human height, with some accounts giving heights of thirteen to fifteen feet or more.

Other accounts of giant finds include a 15-foot human skeleton found in southeast Turkey in the late 1950's in the Euphrates valley during road construction. In AD 235 a giant Maximinus Thrax Ceaser became the emperor of the Roman Empire between 235-238 A.D. . His skeleton was 8'6" skeleton. Biblical accounts of giants include Goliath who was about 9 feet in the late 11th century, according to Samuel 17:4 and King Og who was approximately 14'6" cited in Deuteronomy 3:11. A 19'6" human skeleton was found in 1577 A.D. under an overturned oak tree in the Canton of Lucerne. A 23-foot tall skeleton was allegedly found in 1456 A.D. beside a river in Valence, France. A 25' 6 " skeleton was found in 1613 A.D. near the castle of Chaumont in France. And finally, allegedly two separate 36-foot human remains uncovered by Carthaginians who allegedly lived between 200-600 B.C

Bust of Maximinus Thrax who rose to power due to his 8 foot tall stature

Although there really are only a few accounts of actual giant skeletons being found, some websites want us to assume that everyone living between 1700-1830 were giant. They post pictures of giants that lived after 1830 for proof that they existed before 1830. Here is an example of one such post:

Descendant of the Giants, 1925.

This photograph was taken by Martin Chambi Jimenez, one of the first famous photographers among Latin America. He was recognized for the deep historical and ethnic documentary value of his photographs.

The photo shows a tall man, native of the southern highlands of Paruro province and the photographer himself. This race of tall people lived in some parts of the Amazon forests not more than a few centuries ago.

Skeletons found in those locations "show no signs of diseases such as hormonal growth problems that are common in most cases of gigantism. On all skeletons, the joints were healthy, and the lung cavity was large. Most skeletons have all signs of old age and natural death from old age, according to the British anthropologist Russell Dement.

These claims of giants seem fantastic! The pictures look like real giants! But, when you analyze the photos, you will see that the giants are often shown leaning onto the person next to them. Or their hands look enormous and disproportionate to the rest of their body, as if they have an environmental or congenital issue with their pituitary gland rather than being a natural giant genetically. Or the photo is fake and photoshopped.

Those who believe giants existed in our recent past point to the enormous proportions of older buildings such as cathedrals or gilded mansions, which they say were actually built earlier in history. Doors to these structures seem gigantic. Two examples that are frequently posted on the internet are the door to San Giovanni, a basilica in Rome, and the entrance to the Pantheon in Italy. As they say, the meek shall inherit the earth.

Door from San Giovanni in Laterano [105]

Entrance to The Pantheon, Rome, Italy [106]

Many websites and youtube videos post giant objects that could have been used by giant people like giant books, swords, tools, and musical instruments.

Ancient art often depicts giants. Maybe this was just an art form and not meant to be taken literally. But these pictures make you wonder.

Ancient mural painting in the Nubian pyramids depicting a Giant carrying two elephants.

Egyptian images portraying varying sizes of people next to giants

The Nephilim

Mythological stories of giants are prevalent in various cultures throughout history, including the Bible, Quran, and Greek and Roman mythology. These tales are found in oral history, folklore, literature, and movies. The Book of Enoch speaks of fallen angels who interbred with humans and produced giant offspring known as the Nephilim. The canonical Bible also mentions the Nephilim as the mighty ones of old.

The Sons of God Saw the Daughters of Men That They Were Fair [107\]

The Nephilim are figures mentioned in the Hebrew Bible and various other ancient texts. In the Bible, they are described as the offspring of the "sons of God" and the "daughters of men." The exact nature and identity of the "sons of God" is a matter of debate, with various interpretations suggesting that they were fallen angels or other divine beings.

The Nephilim are often portrayed as giants or superhuman beings, possessing great strength and power. Some myths suggest that they were responsible for teaching humans various skills and technologies, while others portray them as violent and destructive forces that ultimately led to the downfall of humanity. The Nephilim were considered a destructive force, full of corruption and wickedness. They were said to have corrupted human genetics and destroyed the Earth. The Bible describes the Earth as being filled with violence before the Great Flood, which was created by God to rid the Earth of the Nephilim and save humanity. Noah survived the flood because his genetics had not been corrupted by the Nephilim.

The myth of the Great Flood can be found in various cultures around the world, including Hebrew, Hindu, Babylonian, Norse, Chinese, African, European, Mesoamerican, Mesopotamian, and Australian Aborigine. The myth has been mythologized and fragmented, but there is one true historical account of what happened before and during the flood. The account has been deliberately manipulated to deceive and confuse people. The truth can be suppressed and manipulated through the narrative.

If giants existed, why do they hide this from us? Some mud flood theorists like EWAR theorized it would destroy people's belief in the theory of evolution.

Were We Once Breatharians Without the Need to Use the Toilet?

The Tartaria theory suggests that there were no bathrooms in old buildings. Historical revisionists use examples such as the Palace of Versailles, which has no toilets, to support this claim.

According to mainstream articles, the lack of toilets resulted in a foul odor inside these buildings, and residents and servants would go in the hallway or have containers in their rooms for waste. However, some Tartarian theorists argue that if people went through all the trouble of building such beautiful structures, they must have had bathrooms and running water.

Others suggest that humans may have occupied different bodies at the time these structures were built and absorbed nutrition through the aether, like their fireplaces or wireless appliances. Some Tartarian theorists even point out that the phrase "brethren" used in Freemasonry sounds like "Breatharian" as described by Yogis, who do not rely on food or water for sustenance but on air alone.

Other Mud Flood theorists are not willing to stretch their imagination that far and believe that there must have been some form of bathrooms that have been forgotten. Some researchers have noted structures protruding out of castles called Garderobes, which eliminated waste through a low-tech method by letting it fall into a moat beside the castle. Mud flood theorists also observe that these garderobes appear to have been built later and have mismatched stone.

108

So why were there no bathrooms in these beautiful old buildings? Did they simply use chamber pots, garderobes, or outhouses? Were people literally breatharians back then? Or did they use a different type of toilet we forgot about?

Are Different Races Engineered Between Resets?

According to Theosophists, our species is evolving under the guidance of ascended masters. They propose that we have evolved from minerals to budding asexual cells, then to vegetables, animals, and humans. In the future, they believe our evolution will transform us to spiritual or ethereal beings known as Gods. Theosophists also believe ascended masters are guiding the evolution of seven root races for our Earth. According to Blavatsky, every age creates a new root race, and every age contains seven sub-races. So far, only five root races have appeared, starting from the Polarian to the Hyperborean, Lemurian, Atlantean, and Aryan races. The Atlantean race was divided into seven subraces, including the Rmoahal, Cro-Magnons, Toltec, Turanian, Semitic, Akkadian, and Mongolian, with descendants of Atlanteans believed to include American Indians, Turks, Semites, and Mongolians.

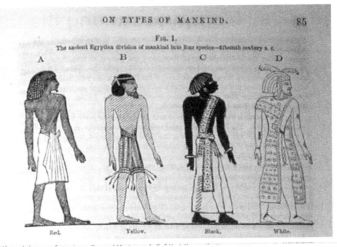

ON TYPES OF MANKIND. 85
Fig. 1.
The ancient Egyptian division of mankind into four species—fifteenth century B.C.

A   B   C   D

Red.   Yellow.   Black.   White.   103

The fifth root race are Aryans. According to Theosophists, the subraces of the Aryan Fifth Root Race include the Hindus, the Arabians, the Persians, the Celts, the Mycenean Greeks, the Germans, and German offshoots known as the Slavs. According to Blavatsky the sixth subrace of the Aryan root race would begin to evolve in the area of the United States in the early 21st century. According to Manly Hall in his book "The Seven Races of Mankind from Atlantis", a race cannot evolve from a homogenous group of people, but from a polyglot that lives over a large area.

Is there a connection between Blavatsky's root race theory and the promotion of interracial relationships in the United States with the goal of increasing diversity within the white community? Are there social engineering initiatives intended to create a new sixth subrace within the Aryan root race? A recent Brookings Institute study predicts that by 2045, the population in the United States will be split approximately 1/2 White, 1/4 Latino, 1/8 Black, and 1/16 Asian, presenting a neatly engineered set of ratios for an upcoming reset. Will this future mixed-race be bred from a perfect balance of half-white individuals, or will it come from those who resist mixing and remain 100% white?

Maybe Blavatsky is just another disinformation artist. Perhaps all the root races she describes have already existed. Perhaps they release a variety of brown, yellow, and white pawns each age. Maybe more docile races are being created today. This may continue until we approach another golden age, only to repeat the cycle once more.

Is There Genetic Re-Engineering Via Clones Between Resets?

According to some mud flood theorists, cloning occurs during resets. And Cabbage Patch Machines giving birth to babies really existed during the 1880s. Could humans who die during a reset could potentially become the source of DNA for clones? Could their DNA be combined with "patch software updates" by an unknown controlling entity.

It is unclear what the implications would be for individuals who survive a reset, especially if they choose to live off the grid. They may miss out on the supposed software updates that occur during the death and rebirth process, if such a process indeed exists.

Are there Arranged Marriages Among the Elite after Reset?

Were upper class marriages arranged between cousins after Reset? Did this help re-engineer human DNA?

Perhaps human genetics is manipulated during Resets so that we become genetically similar. Either through cloning or arranged marriages. Genetically similar people might be more likely to form high trust societies.

According to a geology study, the relatedness between couples increased between 1825 and 1875, despite railway travel. After 1875, partners became less related. [109] Why did this occur during the Reset period proposed by Mud Flood theorists? Is that part of the arrangement if one is to survive reset?

In parts of Ancient Greece, first-cousin marriage was not only allowed but encouraged, DNA shows.

Ancient Melted Cities

Were ancient cities melted by fiery natural disasters or nuclear weapons? Was there a plasma storm event that heated earth's structures in the past? Did the elite pour geopolymer or cement facades on top of melted, brick ruins to disguise them as cliffs or mountains? Mud Flood theorists have considered all these theories. They call this topic Meltology.

Many similar melted-looking structures are found throughout the world. When historians find these muddy structures near the ocean, they call them cliffs or natural formations. If historians find these structures in the Middle East, they call them carved structures. Sometimes archaeologists claim these structures were made of adobe brick or mud brick.

Let's examine some of them.

Bandelier National Monument in New Mexico

Melted Structure, or Carved into rock? The Bandelier National Monument in New Mexico contains dwellings that Native Americans carved into soft rock cliffs. These dwellings are called petroglyphs. Visitors can go to this site and see little rooms inside these cliffs.

111

One interesting aspect of these monuments is the brick-like sections, which some believe were added during reconstruction. However, according to mud flood theorists, these bricks suggest that the ruins were once melted, brick buildings. It's possible that a fiery disaster exposed the old brick structures to intense heat, causing parts of the building to melt and exposing the bricks that once made up the structure. Perhaps the buildings were covered with ash or plasma that dripped over the entire structure during the disaster. After the disaster, people could have drilled out holes into the cliff to create cheap shelters.

If ancient people carved these structures, why would they leave incomplete divots in the structures that don't lead inside the rock?

Is Bandelier National Monument: Carved into Rock or Melted?

110

Cappadocia Turkey

Melted Structure or carved into rock?

Cappadocia, Turkey also has many structures that look melted. People of the villages in the Cappadocia Region carved out houses, churches and monasteries from the soft rocks of volcanic deposits. The town Göreme within the Cappadocia region became a monastic center in 300–1200 AD.

112

The ancient church Açik Saray is pictured above. The name means Open Palace. Ancient people allegedly carved this structure into the valley walls in Gülşehir, Cappadocia However, individual stones or bricks seem to be lie underneath an orange facade. The top of the structure looks completely cooked and puffed up. The structure looks as if it were topped with some sort of ash which was flowing down the roof, dripping like hot wax.   The openings to the building seem inconsistent - some are perfect arches while others are rough rectangles. Was this structure once a normal looking stone structure that survived a fiery disaster?

Le Rocce Rosse di Arbatax

Natural Formation or Melted Brick Structure?

Le Rocce Rosse di Arbatax Raggiungerle is supposed to be a natural rock formation by the beach in Italy. It translates into Red Rocks Bay. Why does it have bricks? Was this once a brick structure melted in a natural disaster?

113

Some mud flood theorists think perhaps a geopolymer was poured over brick structures to disguise them as natural formations. A geopolymer is a type of material that can be made by mixing various minerals, such as clay, limestone, and volcanic ash, with an alkaline solution to create a chemical reaction that forms a hard substance similar to stone.

The Palace Tomb, Petra

Carved in Rock, or Melted in Rock?

114

The Royal Tombs of Petra embody the unique artistry of the Nabateans while also giving display to Hellenistic architecture, but the façades of these tombs have worn due to natural decay. These toms were carved into the Sandstone in the earth.

Mud Flood theorists ask: Was this carved, or was rock melted over it? If it was carved, why have incomplete windows on top? Why not finish the job?

Ruined castle in Ogrodzieniec

Collapsed or Melted?

115

Ogrodzieniec Castle is a ruined medieval castle in Podzamcze, near Ogrodzieniec, the south-central region of Poland called Polish Jura. Originating in the 14th century the castle was rebuilt several times in its long history. It is situated on the top of 1691 foot high Castle Mountain, the highest hill of the Kraków-Częstochowa Upland. The ruins are open to visitors and are a part of Trail of the Eagles' Nests, a hiking trail that connects a number of well known castles in the region.

People who believe in Resets believe Ogrodzieniec Castle was melted by a fiery disaster. Such as a plasma storm. This disaster could have been natural, or caused by directed energy weapons. Mud flood theorists note how the castles with individual stones and bricks seems to merge with amorphous stone.

Castle of the English in Bouzies, 14th century

Built into a Cliff, or Smothered By Melting Rock?

The Castle of the English in Bouzies, 14th century.

The Château des Anglais is a castle in the commune of Autoire in the Lot département of France. The castle extends under a rocky cliff, partially overhanging, which limits its area. The English castle of Bouziès is located high up, on the road to Cahors in Saint-Cirq Lapopie, in the cliff. You can see fortifications from the 14th and 15th centuries, anchored in the limestone rock. The Château des Anglais served as a refuge to protect the population in the event of an attack. One can observe how a rounded tower on the bottom left seems to merge with the rock above it. Why would it be built this way?Could the castle have been smothered in a melting cliff during a past reset?

Western Deffufa of Kerma

Primitive Mud Brick Construction, or Melted Structure?

Pictured above is Western Deffufa of Kerma. The word Defuffa is either the Nubian word for a mud-brick building or the Arabic word daffa, meaning pile. There are only three deffufa remaining in the world. They are located at the former site of the Nubian Kingdom of Kerma. The Nubian kingdom existed between 2500 and 1500 B.C.

The remains of the walled city of Kerma is one of the largest archaeological sites in ancient Nubia. Archaeologists have identified a system of roads and well-differentiated neighborhoods. It is likely that this metropolis was reserved for members of the royal elite and the ruling class.

Houses in Kandovan, Iran

Carved in volcanic rock, or buried in melting rock?

117

Kandovan is an ancient village in northwestern Iran. At the 2006 census, the population was 601. The village consists of manmade cliff dwellings which are still inhabited, we are told. The troglodyte homes, excavated inside volcanic rocks are similar to dwellings in the Turkish region of Cappadocia. The cone form of the houses is the result of the erosion of ignimbrite layers consisting of porous, round and angular pumice together with other volcanic particles that were positioned in a gray, acidic matrix. During the eruption of Sahand, pyroclastic flows formed the rocks of Kandovan. Around the village the thickness of this formation exceeds 330 ft and with time, due to water erosion, the cone-shaped cliffs were formed.

It is interesting that these houses were allegedly carved in volcanic rock, when you can clearly observe individual bricks inside the structure.

The City of Setenil in Spain

Built under a Rock, or Melted Under a Rock?

118

T   The city of Setenil in Spain is one of the strangest cities in the world. Its inhabitants live under the largest rock in the world since it was built by the Muslims in the days of Andalusia. Residents there enjoy a cold in the summer and warm in the winter, because the roofs of their homes are the same rock that prevents the penetration of heat or coldness.

Were these buildings built under a rock, or did the rock melt over these buildings during a past fiery disaster?

1904 World's Fair Exhibit called "Cliff Dwellers"

Are Melted Structures Easily Manmade?

      This is a 1904 World's Fair Exhibit called "Cliff Dwellers". The exhibit was a reproduction of Battle Rock Mountain, Colorado. Does this exhibit indicate that many 'natural formations' are actually old, melted buildings with Staff poured on top? Was a geopolymer poured over a house-shaped structure to create a cliff?

      Many Mud Flood theorists who believe geopolymer was poured over brick structures to form fake mountains are forming a movement called "Boots on the Ground". They explore their own local areas to see if they can find proof that brick structures are found under many so-called natural formations. The youtube channel iRS MEDIA shared a video showing unidentified brick ruins off the side of a California Highway. Other channels show people literally digging into cliffs with axes, and finding perfect red bricks buried underneath muddy cliffs. Are these all hoax videos, or are there really buried, melted structures underneath faux rock facades?

Pompeii Bodies:

Mummified or Plastered?

Pompeii was an ancient city located near Naples in Italy. The volcano Mount Vesuvias erupted in 79 A.D., and buried Pompeii and its citizens with 13 to 20 ft of volcanic ash and pumice.

Thereafter, archaeologists allegedly found the bodies. Somehow, the bodies weren't instantly incinerated to ashes.

Children from the 80s may remember being told that these bodies were "mummified" by the lava, and that archaeologists discovered the bodies already mummified. A 1960s photograph below shows archaeologists pretending to un-bury 'mummified 'bodies with axes. There are no plaster kits on site.

However, archaeologists now say they found voids in the ash that could be used as molds to make plaster. The voids served as casts to create figures representing people in their final moments.

Which narrative is right Mainstreamers? Were these bodies found mummified, or did you plaster holes you found inside the ash? Decide on your narrative! Stop changing it!

119

False unburying aside, Pompeii was burnt. And one can roam a few abandoned streets of Pompeii to see what the architectural style was like back then. Many people note that the ancients used three to four layers of brick to construct their buildings. These types of brick buildings can be found all over the world, as the Roman empire must have been global. Pompeii was likely near the center of the global civilization at the time of a worldwide fire event. Perhaps this enhanced history helps us visualize how the people lived, and what happened to the entire globe. Perhaps the fire in Pompeii was not localized or caused by a volcano, but was a global plasma event.

What Caused The Melting Event?

According to a mud theorist online, the 1587 map shows the world before the great plasma event. Then the plasma event occurred. It was caused by the return of Satan symbolized by the lightning bolt. A Saturnian lightning bolt struck the earth superheating and melting all the buildings that we have seen the proof of. The heat vaporized all of the water in the soil as well as any rivers or lakes near the areas struck. The superheated steam rose high into the atmosphere and spread across the world. This steam condensed and fell, causing torrential rains. These torrential rains triggered the mudfloods worldwide. The poles froze with snow and ice. Wooly mammoths were frozen in their tracks, creating the impression of an ice age.

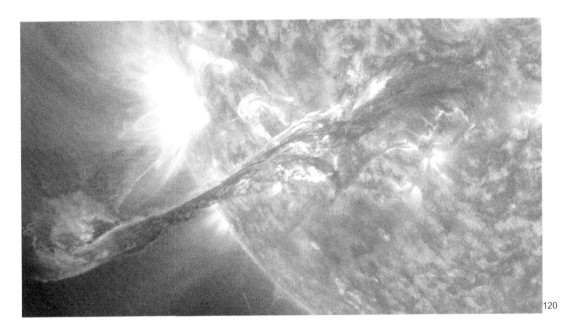
120

Did Our Ancestors Work With Geopolymers?

The idea of "Tartarian" advanced civilizations creating structures using a form of melted geopolymer is a controversial topic that is not supported by mainstream archaeologists and historians.

Geopolymer is a type of material that can be made by mixing various minerals, such as clay, limestone, and volcanic ash, with an alkaline solution to create a chemical reaction that forms a hard substance similar to stone. Some proponents of the "Tartarian" theory suggest that ancient civilizations used this method to create structures that appear to have been carved out of solid rock. Or perhaps some ancient art was not carved marble, but a melted geopolymer allowed to cool inside a cast.

Was this stone wall of Nijo-jo, Japan created by melting and pouring a geopolymer into a mold, or quarrying and lifting heavy rocks?

Veiled Lady, Artist Corradini. Was this statue made by melting and pouring a geopolymer into a cast, or hand-carved out of marble?

123

Were these petroglyph handprints created by carving into rock? Or from melting a geopolymer, and sliding a hand through the mixture when wet?

Why do adobe structures have bricks peeking through a clay facade? Was a geopolymer poured over the ruins of old brick buildings to create faux adobe buildings?

Star Cities

Tartarian theorists are obsessed with bastion star forts, and star villages. These walled cities and forts were usually cannon-resistant, and were popular in the 16th and 17th centuries. Not only are they found all over Western Europe, like Portugal and the Netherlands, but also far away in Asia and in Sri Lanka. About 90% of the time, these Star Forts are attributed to the Spanish and Portuguese colonists. When one studies a map of star forts attributed to the Spanish and Portuguese, they realize that they got around! It seems impossible for a small group of white boys to have traveled the world and built all this while conquering natives and figuring out how to eat in a foreign land.

Fort Bourtange [124]

Mainstream historians claim the Spanish and Portuguese built these forts and walled cities to withstand cannon fire.

The star shape provided several advantages over earlier fortification designs which were rectangular or circular.

One of the main advantages of the star shape was that it allowed for greater visibility and fields of fire. The bastions or projecting sections of the fortification allowed for the placement of artillery and soldiers, providing overlapping fields of fire and allowing defenders to fire upon attacking forces from multiple angles.

Mud Flood theorists simply do not believe these advanced structures were solely built for military use to withstand cannon fire. Often, villages for civilians were placed within these stars.

Most forts had an advanced moat system, which were often drained and hidden later. Many mud flood theorists claim you can find valves or drains on these moat systems. Often tunnels are found in or around the fort system. They believe that the entire globe was connected not only via railroads and roads, but via a water-based infrastructure. And that the flow of water was tapped for the use in generating electricity.

The town of Palmanova, Italy, was built as a star fort by the Venetian Republic in 1593 [125]

These star forts are usually located on the coast. It seems that if a ship firing upon the enemy really wanted to invade land, they would just sail around these forts.

Were There Castles in America?
Were many destroyed by a Fiery Disaster?

Are castles found all over the earth? Were castles a common style for buildings in a past reset? Many structures that look like castles look like they suffered a fiery reset. The castles below are found in North America.

Cliff Palace at Mesa Verde

Is Cliff Palace at Mesa verde really a ruin from the Pueblo people, or an ancient castle? Many people believe the ruins of Mesa Verde in Colorado look similar to various castles found in Europe. Perhaps the United States had castles like Europe, and these castles were destroyed by an ancient EMP attack.

126

American Castle at Ha Ha Tonka State Park:

America Castle at Ha Ha Tonka State Park in Missouri. The official story is that Robert McClure Snyder, Sr., a Kansas City businessman, constructed the Ha Ha Tonka castle in 1905. Following Snyder's death in an auto accident in 1906, the castle was completed by his sons Robert Jr., LeRoy, and Kenneth Snyder in the early 1920s. In the late 1930s, it was used as a hotel. It was destroyed by fire in 1942. Perhaps the official story is untrue, and this is actually an ancient relic in the United States built before an 1830s reset.

127

The castle is situated on a bluff overlooking the Lake of the Ozarks and features stunning architecture, including a central courtyard with a large fountain, a grand staircase, and numerous stone archways and towers. Visitors can take guided tours of the castle's interior, which includes a ballroom, dining room, and numerous bedrooms and living spaces. The castle also offers spectacular views of the surrounding landscape and is a popular spot for photography.

Coral Castle at Miami

Coral Castle, Homestead, Florida[128]

Coral Castle is a unique stone structure located in Homestead, Florida, which is about 25 miles south of Miami. The structure was built by a Latvian-American man named Edward Leedskalnin between 1923 and 1951.

Leedskalnin began construction on Coral Castle in the early 1920s, using blocks of coral rock that he quarried himself from a nearby site. He worked alone, using simple tools and techniques to cut, shape, and move the massive stone blocks, some of which weighed as much as 30 tons. Leedskalnin's methods remain something of a mystery, as he was famously secretive about his construction techniques and never allowed anyone to watch him work.

Despite the enormous scale of the project, Leedskalnin built Coral Castle entirely by himself and without the use of any machinery. He eventually created an entire complex of structures, including a castle tower, a sundial, a fountain, and a series of stone tables and chairs.

After Leedskalnin's death in 1951, the site was turned into a tourist attraction and has remained one ever since.

Other castles in United States:

Belvedere Castle, Central Park in New York City - built in 1865

Bannerman Castle, by Hudson River in New York STate - a Scottsman built in in 1901

Castello Di Amorosa - in Napa Valley, California, winery opened to public 2007

Montezuma Castle, Camp Verde, Arizona, constructed by Singua people 800 years ago

Lyndhurst Castle, Hudson River, constructed 1838

Loveland Castle in Loveland, Ohio

Overlook Castle in Asheville, North Carolina

Conquistadors, Colonizers, and Crusaders:

False Narratives for a Global Genetic reset?

A few thugs from Spain and Portugal arrive in South America. These conquistadors knock up all the women. They build star forts, aqueducts, cathedrals, roads, tunnels everywhere. They teach all the mixed children Spanish. They convert the country to Catholicism. Today, South Americans have about 45% European ancestry.[128]

Similarly, European colonizers established colonies in North America and decimated the population there. They took most of the land and resources.

Is this true, or was there a Mudflood reset which involved genetic changes in certain populations?

Similarly, European colonizers established colonies in Asia, African, and Oceania. They fought Crusades in the Middle East. They displaced the native populations everywhere and led them to significant cultural changes. These places gained neoclassical style architecture and new technology. But the native populations lost land, resources, and their cultural heritage. How would entire countries allow themselves to be dominated by a few pale skinned people demanding to be serviced? Is the theme of conquistadors, colonizers, and crusaders just the mainstream narrative designed to cover up the phenomenon of global resets involving altered architecture, culture, and genetics?

Ancient Reset: Giants and the Great Flood

Were Enormous Living Things Petrified in the Distant Past?
Did a Great Flood occur as described in the Bible?

Every culture has a flood myth. Abrahamic religions have Noah's flood. The Mayans have the Hutacon flood where the word hurricane comes from. Ancient Hawaiians have the Newton flood. The Sumerians wrote about a flood in Gilgamesh, Europe. Asia Pacific Islanders and native tribes from All Over America they all talk about a great flood that cleansed the Earth so civilization could start again.

In the Bible, the Great Flood was created by God to cleanse the Earth of wickedness and the Nephilim. According to Abrahamic religions, the Nephilim were the result of the union between the "sons of God" and the daughters of Adam. They were often referred to as "the fallen ones" or "the dead ones" and were known as great biblical giants. They were so wicked and evil that God saw the need to destroy them, and thus created the Great Flood as a means to do so.

Mud Flood theorists believe giants and giant living things existed in the distant past. Some even believe these life forms were silicone-based rather than carbon-based, and were turned to stone during a mega-disaster. They call the event that destroyed these living things "Medusa".

Medusa is a figure from Greek mythology. She was a Gorgon, a creature with snakes for hair and the ability to turn people to stone with her gaze. The story of Medusa is most famously told in the Greek myth of Perseus, who was tasked with killing her and used her head as a weapon. She turned men to stone by looking them in the eye. So she could not be touched or seen. And her petrifying gaze could kill anyone who looked at her. This made her a goddess of war. She killed many soldiers during the Trojan War.

Perhaps there is some truth to the legend of Medusa. Maybe some sort of plasma event linked to the sun caused life forms to turn to stone, and this event could be called "Medusa". Thereafter, similar types of events occur every 250-300 years to Reset life on earth. Others believe that a great flood occurred just once to flood out giants, and that holy books such as the Bible are just a misinterpreted book of human history.

Mountains, or Huge Petrified Trees?

Mud Flood theorists often share pictures that look like enormous tree stumps, or giants turned to stone.

Devils tower looks like an enormous tree stump. [133] However, mainstream geologists say it is a hill composed of igneous rock in Wyoming.

The village of Amedye, Iraq. Looks like it is built upon a giant tree. [134]

What if Mountains are Just Sleeping Giants?

Myths and legends that claim mountains are actually sleeping giants have been passed down in some cultures for centuries. Were these the Nephilm? Were they silicone life forms that were somehow petrified and turned into stone in a disaster? Maybe the Hills have Eyes!

      Pictured here are Ceuta, Sleeping Lady Mountain (Top Left)[135,] (Top Right) The Grey Man of the Merrick, Scotland (Top Right)[136,] The Great Stone Face Rock, Pennington Gap, VA (Middle Left),[137] Peña de los Enamorados Antequera, Malaga (Middle Right)[138], Old Man of the park. Near Sundance, Wyo, (Bottom Left)[139,] (Bottom Right) Old Man of the Mountain, New Hampshire (Bottom Right)[140]

Mountains that Look like Animals

Many mud flood theorists are fascinated with rock formations that look like giant animals. Are these mountains proof of a phenomenon known as the "Medusa Effect" which caused living organisms to turn into stone?

Elephant Rock in Iceland[141]

Hvitserkur, Iceland, looks like a Rhinoceros[142]

Did a Genetic Study Show that 90% of Earth's Animals Appeared at the Same Time?

Some Mud Flood theorists point to a recent genetic study for proof that there was some "Noah's Ark" release of animals into the wild 200,000 years ago. A scientific paper published in the journal Human Evolution concludes that a lot of animal species experienced a significant population bottleneck, wherein only a small number of animals survived from over 200,000 years ago.[129] The authors stated that the genetic diversity observed in mitochondrial genomes of most species alive today can be attributed to the accumulation of mutations from an ancestral genome within the past 200,000 years. The paper found that the genetic diversity of mitochondrial DNA is relatively low, about 0.2%, within most animal species, regardless of the species' population size and geographic range. But that the extant population of most species, regardless of their similarity to fossils of any age or current population size, has expanded from mitochondrial uniformity within the past 200,000 years. [130]

Many people conclude that 90% of animal species appeared at the same time as humans, as was reported in some media outlets. However, mainstream scientists claim these findings do not contradict evolutionary theory, and it just means there were significant population bottlenecks.[131]

Perhaps Noah's Ark is merely an allegory for celestial beings manipulating Earth's genetic makeup. In the Bible, Noah was a man who lived around 4,000 years ago and was chosen by God to build an ark in preparation for a great flood that God planned to send to the earth. According to the story, God instructed Noah to gather two of every kind of animal, one male and one female, and bring them onto the ark to preserve them during the flood. The purpose of this was to save the animals from the destruction that would come with the flood and to allow them to repopulate the earth once the floodwaters receded.

Ancient alien theorists believe Noah's Ark is an allegory for saving samples of plant and animal DNA in a spaceship lab before destruction of life on earth, so that the specimens could be distributed on earth later to repopulate the planet after a fallout event.

132

Various Conspiracy Theories That May Shed Light on Resets

If our world is subjected to resets and reboots, what could cause such events? One must delve into the current world of conspiracy theories to explain our conspiracy past!

Let's examine all the conspiracies. Let's dive into the trash in our search for treasure. We'll sift through a veritable junkyard of theories and claims, from flat earth to extraterrestrial life, from genetic engineering to shadow governments, from FEMA camps to secret societies, and from cloning to mind control. Perhaps we will find pearls of wisdom buried within thick piles of dung.

Are you ready to challenge your beliefs?

Truth Buried Within the Flat Earth Movement

Why is the Mud Flood Reset Theory always combined with the outlandish Flat Earth theory on the Internet? Do Flat Earthers have any Truths to Offer?

You cannot read about the Reset Theory on the internet without being exposed to topics like Flat Earth, Bible Prophecy, "Tartaria" and Giants from the 19th Century. Perhaps Secret Societies disperse truth, but always combine the truth with disinformation or topics that do not seem credible. This would make the mainstream scoff at the truth. If they only give us half-truths, it would be up to us and our spiritual evolution to find our own truth. Maybe you cannot understand Reset Theory without extracting the truth from these other Far-Out Theories like Flat Earth.

Flat Earth Theory proposes that the Earth is Flat with a Dome shaped firmament above it, and all the planets are merely "luminaries" that are embedded in or above the top of the dome.

144

Ancient Belief Systems that Supported Flat Earth Theory

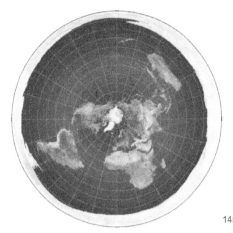

145

Flat Earthers claim we should believe the Earth was flat because ancient people believed this was the case. They cite ancient belief systems that support their theory. Many ancient cultures, including the Babylonians, Egyptians, and Mesopotamians, believed in a flat Earth that was often depicted as a disc or plane, with the sky or heavens above it. This view was based on observations of the horizon and the apparent flatness of the Earth's surface, as well as on religious and mythological beliefs about the structure of the cosmos.

For example, in ancient Egypt, the Earth was believed to be a flat, rectangular object, surrounded by water, with the sky above it. This belief was reflected in their art and religious texts, which often depicted the Earth as a flat surface with the sun, moon, and stars moving across the sky.

Similarly, in Mesopotamia, the Earth was often depicted as a flat, circular disc surrounded by water, with the sky or heavens above it. This view was based on observations of the horizon and the apparent flatness of the Earth's surface, as well as on religious and mythological beliefs about the structure of the cosmos.

In bible cosmology, God created the firmament as a vast solid dome to divide the primal sea into upper and lower portions so that dry land could appear. The ancient Hebrews, like all the ancient peoples of the Near East, believed the sky was a solid dome with the Sun, Moon, planets and stars embedded in it.

Overall, while there were some ancient cultures that believed in a round Earth, such as the ancient Greeks, this view was not widely accepted until much later in history. Many cultures held beliefs in a flat Earth based on their observations of the natural world and their religious and mythological beliefs.

Around the 4th to 3rd centuries BCE, Aristotle argued that the heavens must be perfect and that a sphere was the perfect geometrical figure. Consequently, the Greeks exchanged the Flat Earth concept for a spherical Earth surrounded by solid spheres. This became the dominant model in the Classical and Medieval world-view, and even when Copernicus placed the Sun at the center of the system he included an outer sphere that held the stars.

The Moon Landing Was Faked!!

Flat earthers point out that the moon landing seems fake. But just because the moon landing could have been faked does not mean the earth is flat. Here's a summary of why it seems fake is as follows:

1. The flag waved on the moon: During the first moon landing, viewers observed the American flag waving as Neil Armstrong and Buzz Aldrin planted it. However, this poses a problem as there is no air on the moon to cause such movement.

2. Funky Shadows: On the moon there is only one strong light source: the Sun. So it's fair to suggest that all shadows should run parallel to one another. But this was not the case during the moon landing. Videos and photographs clearly show that shadows fall in different directions

3. The Van Allen Radiation Belt: To reach the moon, astronauts had to pass through the Van Allen radiation belt. This is an area with high radiation levels that would have been lethal to humans. The sheer levels of radiation would have cooked the astronauts en route to the moon, despite the layers of aluminum coating the interior and exterior of the spaceship.

4. The footage was filmed in slow motion: In order to create the effect of weak gravity on the moon, the astronauts were carried by thin wires and filmed jumping around. NASA then slowed down the film, according to the conspiracy theorists, in order to make it look like they were floating through the air. If you slow the footage 2.5X, it looks normal as if it were filmed on earth.

5. No Stars: In the photographic and video evidence of the moon landing, no stars are visible. This is suspicious as stars are always present in the moon's sky.

6. The "C" rock: One of the photos from the moon landing shows a rock with a symmetrical "C" engraved into it, which some claim is evidence of a prop.

7. How do you film the Lunar Module leaving the moon? Somehow the astronauts on board filmed the Lunar Module leaving the moon's surface, and retrieved the footage for all to see later. Mainstream historians claim the camera was somehow mounted to the Lunar Module , and remotely controlled by mission control on earth. That's even more interesting! How did they control a camera remotely from earth in the 1960s?

8. Nixon called the moon on the phone: On July 20, 1969, President Richard Nixon literally placed an out-of-this-world phone call when he rang-up the Apollo 11 astronauts on the moon. Mainstream historians claim this was possible because the call was placed through a NASA radio transmitter.

9. The Stanley Kubrick confession: Acclaimed film director Stanley Kubrick was approached by the US government to hoax the first three moon landings. A video emerged after his death where he admitted this.

Why could they fake the moon landing? Money? Fame? Who knows! But it seems we've been lied to.

Conflicting Globe CGI Images:

Do our modern scientists have the real truth? Our modern scientists point to satellite pictures or photographs we have of the globe from space. However, it is interesting that all their versions of the globe seem to differ with the size of different continents in relation to the globe. Perhaps we are never given the full truth.

Mainstream astronomers explain that CGI images of Earth can sometimes appear to conflict with the actual size of continents because of the way the images are generated. Most CGI images of Earth are created by wrapping a 2D map of Earth's surface onto a 3D sphere, which can distort the size and shape of continents. This is because 2D maps of Earth are projections of the 3D surface onto a flat surface, and different map projections can result in different distortions. Additionally, the position of the camera and the angle at which the image is taken can also affect the apparent size of the continents in relation to the globe.

You would have thought our NASA scientists would have made the necessary calculations to accurately adjust the 2D map images if they are considered the most scientifically accurate images of the planet.

Illogical Flight Patterns

Flat earthers observe that when travelers take flights from one spot in the northern hemisphere to another, they rarely cross the equator. But if they take a flight from one southern continent to the other, their flights almost always include a connecting flight through the northern hemisphere. Flat earthers claim these commercial flights support the UN flag's layout of earth.

If you were to explain the flight patterns using a round shaped earth, perhaps the earth is bigger, and the continents are arranged on a large round earth in a way that looks like the UN flag, with more continents south of this. However, this would not explain reversed seasons in the southern hemisphere, unless we share the same equator. A book written by Eddie Alencar describes 16 emergency landings on airplane flights that would only make sense on a flat earth's layout of the continents.

The Moon is Visually the Same Size as the Sun on Earth

The Sun and Moon appear to be the same size from Earth's perspective because of a coincidence of their respective sizes and distances. The Sun's diameter is about 400 times larger than the Moon's diameter, but it is also about 400 times farther away from the Earth than the Moon. As a result, when the Moon passes in front of the Sun during a solar eclipse, it can block the Sun's disk almost completely, making it appear as if the two bodies have the same apparent size in the sky. This phenomenon is a rare and spectacular event that has been observed and studied by astronomers for centuries.

Flat Earthers say the chances of this happening randomly are almost impossible, and so therefore something may have "built" the moon.

The Moon is a "Luminary"

Flat earthers note that the moon seems to glow like a light in the sky. Therefore, they consider the Moon to be a luminary, just like the Sun. Flat Earthers believe that the Moon emits its own light rather than reflecting the light of the Sun, which is the scientific consensus. They say that it just cannot be a rock reflecting light in dark space, yet be this bright.

Flat Earthers argue that the Moon's light is cold and does not produce shadows with sharp edges, which they believe is evidence that the Moon's light is not reflected sunlight. However, this claim is not supported by scientific evidence and is not widely accepted by the scientific community.

How Does Water Stick to a Spinning Ball?

According to flat earthers, water could never stick to a spinning ball. A little gravity could not make water stick if it's spinning over 1000 miles per hour.

According to conventional science though, water sticks to the surface of the Earth due to gravity, which is the force of attraction between two objects with mass. The Earth's mass creates a gravitational force that pulls objects towards its center, including water. The centrifugal force caused by the Earth's rotation is not strong enough to overcome gravity and fling water off the surface. Additionally, water is a fluid, which means it can conform to the shape of its container and flow along the contours of the Earth's surface.

The moon always shows its same face to the earth without spinning

Flat earthers consider the Moon as anything as a disc in the sky, because the Moon itself always faces Earth the same way.

Mainstream astronomers say the same face of the Moon always faces Earth because of a phenomenon called tidal locking. Tidal locking occurs when the gravitational force between two objects causes one object to rotate at the same rate that it orbits the other object. In the case of the Moon and Earth, the gravitational forces between the two have caused the Moon to rotate on its axis in the same amount of time that it takes to orbit Earth, which is about 27.3 days. As a result, the Moon always keeps the same face towards Earth, while the other side of the Moon is permanently facing away from Earth.

The Moon's face could be an old map of the Flat World 'burnt in'

Flat Earthers claim that the moon has an image of Earth's land masses 'burnt in 'from an ancient time. They believe they can overlay Earth's continents onto the image of the Moon, and see that there are more continents present on the earth than what we are told.

Mandela Effect and Simulation Theory:

146

      Recently, Simulation Theory and Mandela Effect have become popular on the Internet. The Mandela Effect is a phenomenon in which a large group of people remember an event or a fact differently from how it actually occurred or existed. The term "Mandela Effect " was coined by paranormal researcher Fiona Broome, who noticed that many people believed that Nelson Mandela had died in prison in the 1980s, when in fact he was released in 1990 and went on to become the President of South Africa. Examples of the Mandela Effect include the belief that the Berenstain Bears were actually spelled Berenstein, that the classic children's book series The Bernstein Bears is called The Berenstain Bears, and that the famous line from Star Wars is "Luke, I am your father" when in fact it is "No, I am your father". There are many theories about what causes the Mandela Effect, including alternate realities or timelines, time travel, or even a collective false memory.

      Maybe the cause of the Mandela Effect is that we are in a computer simulation controlled by AI. Conceivably, this computer simulation copies our "Minecraft world" and splits it into two parallel universes for various reasons. If one simulation fails, its players could be transferred to a copy to continue. When there is a glitch during the copy process, AI somehow repairs this glitch with a mistake. For example, perhaps it substitutes "Berenstein Bears" with "Berenstain Bears" when there is a missing character.

      If we are indeed in a Simulation, perhaps part of our round globe is domed off, and we are quarantined away from the rest of the world in our isolated simulation. Perhaps our portion of the domed off earth is a simulation of the real thing with holograms of the stars or moon embedded in our simulated dome.

Dimensional Theory:

Perhaps when we read how other cultures believed in a domed earth or maybe a flat earth, we do not understand how they perceived our reality conceptually. Maybe the ancients did not mean people to take their ideas literally in a physical sense.

Occultists work with sacred geometry and try to reduce 4 dimensional concepts down to 3D or two dimensional drawings. They claim our earth is a hologram. That is, every slice of a portion of it contains the parts of the whole. People who engage in psychedelic drugs claim they see other dimensions. 2D, 3D, 4D, 5D.

Perhaps our earth simply has elements of a two dimensional space as well as a three dimensional and fourth dimensional space.

During occult rituals, the four corners are often called upon as if we are on a plane, and some believe that the Earth is a "plane" rather than a "planet," and that many spirits are from other dimensions. It's possible that all of these beliefs contain some degree of truth and that treating the Earth as flat in certain contexts can help us see reality in a different way.

147

***

Although you may be interested in the Mud Flood Reset Theory, it does not necessarily mean that you also have to believe in the Flat Earth or the idea that Tartaria was the center of an empire in the 1700s. You can still consider these alternative theories without necessarily committing to them. It's important to keep an open mind and consider all the different perspectives and theories that are out there. In a world where truth can be mixed with deception, finding the truth may require sifting through misinformation. So, it's possible to entertain these theories without fully accepting them, which can help you see different truths that are not typically presented by the mainstream narrative. It is the mark of an educated mind to be able to entertain a thought without accepting it. Go ahead! Drink the "Maybe juice".

Was our Earth Created From the Goddess Tiamat?

Or did Earth Come from another Planet which was destroyed?

The Battle of Marduk and Tiamat from Pace of Sennacherib, Nimroud, Nineveh[143]

In ancient Mesopotamian mythology, Tiamat was a goddess of primordial chaos and the personification of the saltwater ocean. According to the Enuma Elish, an epic poem from ancient Babylon, Tiamat and the god Apsu gave birth to the first generation of gods, but the younger gods eventually rebelled against Apsu and killed him. Tiamat was angered by the death of her mate and decided to wage war against the younger gods. She created an army of monsters and dragons to fight for her, but in the end, the god Marduk was able to defeat her and create the world from her body.   Marduk divided her body into two parts: the upper part became the heavens, and the lower part became the earth. He then created humans to inhabit the earth and serve the gods.

Michael Tsarion is an author and public speaker who mentions Tiamat. He has lectured about the destruction of Atlantis by a great flood. He explains how a fiery disaster in space may have created the Great Flood. He claims the water planet Tiamat exploded in space, and many parts of this planet collided with Earth to knock it off its axis. Many of the remnants of Tiamat allegedly make up the asteroid belt today. Tsarion refers to sources such as the Ancient Sumerian Texts, Enuma Elish, The Book of Enoch, including parts left out (Apocryphal books), The Bundahishn, Zecharia Sitchin, Celtic records and legends, channelers, and many suppressed authors.

Maybe there is truth to the phrase "civilization built on the bones of another".

Erich von Däniken's Ancient Astronauts

Did Ancient Astronauts visit our planet and give us advanced technology?

148

Erich von Däniken is a Swiss author and researcher who is best known for his books promoting the theory of ancient astronauts. He suggestes that extraterrestrial beings visited Earth in ancient times and influenced human culture and technology. Erich von Däniken's most famous book is called "Chariots of the Gods".

Von Däniken proposes that extraterrestrial beings visited Earth in ancient times and that they were responsible for many of the technological and cultural advancements of ancient civilizations. He believes that ancient cultures possessed technology that was far more advanced than what was previously believed, and this technology was likely given to humans by extraterrestrial visitors.

Von Däniken demonstrates how many religious texts and myths contain references to extraterrestrial beings, and that these beings were often worshiped as gods by ancient cultures.

Von Däniken argues that many ancient structures, such as the pyramids in Egypt and the stone statues on Easter Island, were constructed with the help of advanced technology that was beyond the capabilities of the humans living at the time. Structures such as the Egyptian pyramids, Stonehenge, and the Moai of Easter Island, and certain artifacts from that period, are products of higher technological knowledge than is presumed to have existed at the times they were manufactured.

Von Däniken also describes ancient artwork throughout the world as containing depictions of astronauts, air and space vehicles, extraterrestrials, and complex technology.

Von Däniken suggests that evidence of extraterrestrial visitation has been intentionally suppressed by governments and other powerful organizations to maintain the status quo.

Zecharia Sitchen and the 12th Planet

Were we seeded from a 12th planet that orbits near our solar system every 3,600 years?

149

Like Daniken, Zecharia Sitchin also believed extraterrestrial beings visited Earth throughout history and played a role in shaping human civilization. Zecharia Sitchin wrote the book series, "The Earth Chronicles,". The first book in the series was called "The 12th Planet". Some of the theories presented by these authors include ancient astronauts who worshiped as gods on earth, ancient technology, and a 12th planet called Nibiru which orbits near the Earth every 3,600 years, and ancient. In his books, Sitchen analyzes Sumerian texts to come up with his theories. According to Sitchen, the Sumerians' writings about their cosmology and history were initially dismissed as myth but should be viewed as history.

The Sumerians lived in ancient Sumer, modern-day Iraq. The Sumerians were the first culture to come out of the Stone Age and had a highly advanced society with education, law, and literature. They were also the first to invent writing and had a sophisticated mathematical system.

Sitchen claims the Sumerian epic of creation called the Enuma Elish is similar to the biblical story of creation. In this epic, Nibiru, a planet in our solar system, collided with another planet called Tiamat approximately four billion years ago. This collision created comets by scattering the lighter outer crust of Tiamat. It also created the asteroid belt by ripping out the inner viscous magma of Tiamat and caused Pluto's unusual orbit by the gravitational influence of Nibiru. Earth is a remnant of a collision between Nibiru and Tiamat.

Sitchen believes that the Sumerian tablets describe the Anunnaki, who were an alien race that came to Earth for gold mining. They landed in Iraq 400,000 years ago, setting up shop in the Tigris Euphrates valley. They decided to genetically engineer the hominoids on Earth to create a slave race to do the work for them. The Annunanki engineered humans to be intelligent enough to serve their creators but not to be their equals. They engineered humans to have a large cerebral cortex size in comparison with other animals on earth.

According to Sitchin, the Anunnaki possessed advanced technology that was far beyond what was available to humans at the time, and that this technology was used to build many of the ancient structures and monuments that exist around the world. Sitchin believed that the Anunnaki were worshiped as gods by ancient cultures, and that many of the world's religions were based on their interactions with humans.

Many scientists who have looked into Sitchen's theories believe that the sudden appearance of sophisticated bacteria on Earth four billion years ago can be explained by this collision. Additionally, many people believe that Earth is unique in the solar system because of its missing crust and plate tectonics, and that these difference could be the result of this planetary collision. Nibiru passed Earth around 200 BC and is expected to orbit back around 3,400 AD, about 1400 years from now.

Sitchen's theories may support the idea of human resets. Perhaps extraterrestrial beings from planets that orbit near our solar system periodically interact with humans on a regular basis during resets, and continue to guide our evolution by genetic engineering.

The Planet X Conspiracy Theorists:

Many conspiracy theorists who followed Zecharia Sitchin's work believed that Nibiru would orbit towards our solar system in 2012.

They believed that Planet X would collide with Earth or pass closely by in 2012 causing catastrophic events such as earthquakes, tsunamis, and the end of the world. This theory gained popularity due to misinterpretations of the ancient Mayan calendar, which some believed predicted the end of the world in 2012.

150

Lloyd Pye and Genetically Engineered Humans

Some theorists such as Lloyd Pye are proponents of Intervention Theory, which posits that humans were genetically engineered by extraterrestrial beings in the distant past. According to Pye, the theory explains various anomalies in human evolution. The sudden appearance of advanced traits, the existence of unexplained gaps in the fossil record, and the absence of a clear evolutionary path from our primate ancestors can all be explained by Intervention Theory.

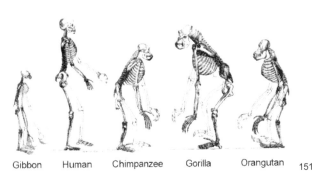

Gibbon   Human   Chimpanzee   Gorilla   Orangutan   151

According to Pye, there was a sudden, drastic change from pre-humans to humans about 100,000 years ago that could not have been accomplished by natural evolution. Anthropologists offer four types of Australopithecus afarensis that existed 3.5-4 million years ago, and two pairs of upright walking chimps existed about 2 million years ago. They tell us there was a natural transition to our homo sapien species. However, when you compare the fossils of the Australopithecus afarensis to the Homo homo, you realize that it would likely require 20-30 million years of natural evolution to accomplish all these changes. Many people, like Lloyd Pye, say this sudden drastic change from Australopithecus afarensis to the Homo genus could only be explained by DNA manipulation in a lab.

The bones of the pre-human Australopithecus afarensis are very different from humans. For instance, Lucy's bone structure is much more robust than that of humans. Her upper arm bone is longer and thicker than that of a human of similar size. Her bones are also said to be more robust in all dimensions compared to humans. Her head is described as that of a chimpanzee. Her arms would be extremely long, and her fingertips would drag near her knees.

According to Pye, Anthropologists, textbooks, and natural history museums are paid to find these pre-human fossils and fudge them every way they can to make them look human. Misleading presentation techniques to depict pre-humans as similar to us include drawing primate-like heads on top of human-like bodies in illustrations, or shortening the skeletons 'arms. Since apes were generally "knuckle draggers", natural history museums prefer to leave off the bottom half of the arms or shorten the arms so people envision the fingertip falling around mid-thigh rather than near the knees. These experts argue that there is not a single human bone in the pre-human fossil record and that the missing link, which would show a smooth transition between pre-humans and humans, has not been found despite over 140 years of searching.

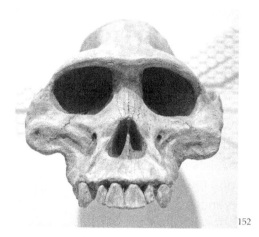

152

Many evolutionary changes from pre-humans to humans happened overnight. These include:
- The shape of the skull, the size and shape of the eyes, the position of the jaw,
- The robustness of the bones. The robustness of the bones is related to the torque the muscles can generate. The Homo species have bones similar to other primates, such as gorillas and chimpanzees, which are much stronger than humans.
- The strength of the muscles. A chimpanzee's musculature is massively stronger than a human's. Chimps could tear the strongest human, like Mike Tyson, up limb for limb
- Human throats are a complete redesign, allowing us to breathe, eat, swallow, and drink simultaneously without choking, whereas primates with their type of throat can make a lot of noise but cannot do what humans can with their throats.
- Pre-humans have different shaped rib cages. They have longer arms and more muscle mass, which requires a bigger fulcrum in the ribcage area to support their movements. This leads to a ribcage that is shaped like an upside-down funnel, as seen in primates. In contrast, modern humans have shorter, lighter arms and bones, and do not require as much muscle mass or a large fulcrum in the ribcage area. Therefore, modern human ribcages have a completely different shape, with an elevated neck that separates the head from the torso.
- Primates have an inability to speak, despite attempts to teach them. They cannot modulate sounds.
- Humans have a larger cerebral cortex size in ratio to their bodies compared with other hominoids and animals
- Humans only have 46 chromosomes. Primates have 48 chromosomes
- Humans have a reverse hair pattern from other primates
- Humans have skin that is different than primates
- Humans have poor night vision

Like Sitchen, Lloyd Pye believes that the Anunnaki was an alien race that came to Earth for gold mining. They landed in Iraq 400,000 years ago, setting up shop in the Tigris Euphrates valley. They decided to genetically engineer the hominoids on Earth to create a slave race to do the work for them. This theory is found in Sumerian myths.

The Annunanki engineered humans to be intelligent enough to serve their creators but not to be their equals. They engineered humans to have a large cerebral cortex size in comparison with other animals on earth.

Lloyd Pye explained the discovery of mitochondrial DNA, and how it showed that all humans have a common ancestor that lived 200-250 thousand years ago in southern Africa. This conflicts with the belief of anthropologists who believed that humans existed for millions of years.

Human defects may prove that we were genetically engineered rather than evolved naturally. Humans have over 4,000 genetic defects, with many severe ones. These defects could be a result of mistakes made during the cutting and splicing process that occurred when humans were genetically engineered by the Anunnaki. Perhaps the Annunanki did not fix these mistakes, because they were focused on creating a slave race rather than producing genetically perfect beings. The genetic defects mentioned by the speaker include spina bifida, which is a birth defect that affects the spine, and mongolism (Down Syndrome), which is a genetic condition characterized by intellectual disability and physical abnormalities.

Humans differ from primates in ways like the Annunaki. Humans only have 46 chromosomes because the Annunanki allegedly only had 46 chromosomes. Primates have 48 chromosomes, but the Anunnaki have only 46 chromosomes. The Annunanki decided to fuse two chromosomes to create a hybrid creature that was a blend of themselves and the creature of Earth. If humans are a hybrid species, the cross could have been between a female ape-like creature and a male person from elsewhere. Like the Annunaki, our muscles are weaker than a chimpanzee. We do not have primate skin. We have a reverse hair pattern from a primate. We have poor night vision. And we have large brains.

Ancient Alien Series

Did Extraterrestrials Visit Earth Throughout History?

"Ancient Aliens" is a television series that explores the theory that extraterrestrial beings have visited Earth throughout history and played a role in shaping human civilization. The show premiered on the History Channel in 2009 and has since become a popular and long-running series.

The show features interviews with experts in archaeology, mythology, and ancient history, as well as UFO enthusiasts and conspiracy theorists. It examines various artifacts, structures, and texts from around the world, and suggests that they may be evidence of ancient astronaut visitation.

The show's main premise is that ancient humans were not capable of building some of the world's most impressive structures on their own, and that these feats must have been accomplished with the help of advanced extraterrestrial technology. The show explores topics such as the construction of the pyramids, the Nazca Lines in Peru, and ancient megalithic structures like Stonehenge.

While "Ancient Aliens" has been criticized by many scholars and experts for promoting pseudoscience and unfounded claims, it remains a popular and entertaining show for those interested in UFOs, ancient mysteries, and conspiracy theories.

Graham Hancock's Ancient Apocalypse Series

Were there Apocalypses and Resets in the Distant Past?

Graham Hancock's Ancient Apocalypse series is a documentary series that explores the possibility that a global cataclysm occurred in the distant past and had a profound impact on human civilization. The series consists of three episodes:

"The Great Flood" explores the story of Noah's Ark and other flood myths from around the world, as well as geological and archaeological evidence that suggests that a massive flood may have occurred around 12,800 years ago.

"The Comet Impact" investigates the theory that a comet impact or series of impacts may have caused the Younger Dryas period of global cooling, which lasted from about 12,900 to 11,700 years ago and had a major impact on human societies.

"The Sunken Kingdom" looks at the myth of Atlantis and other sunken cities and civilizations, as well as evidence for the existence of advanced prehistoric societies that may have been destroyed by a catastrophic event.

Throughout the series, Hancock presents evidence from a range of fields, including geology, archaeology, and mythology, to support his theory that a catastrophic event occurred in the ancient past that shaped the course of human history. While some of his ideas are controversial and have been criticized by other scholars, the Ancient Apocalypse series remains a popular and thought-provoking exploration of the mysteries of our ancient past.

Mud Flooders have a love/hate relationship with Graham Hancock. On the one hand, he supports the idea of human amnesia towards the past and that humanity experiences resets. On the other hand, he claims that these resets could only be ancient. While the mud flood theory proposes that a reset occurred as recently as the 1830s.

What Can Cause a Global Mud Flood?

Many people have theories of how a mud flood was caused, or could have been caused. Many say it's due to a soil liquefaction event, which sometimes happens after an earthquake. Soil liquefaction is a phenomenon that occurs when saturated soil loses its strength and stiffness, causing it to behave like a liquid instead of a solid. This can happen during an earthquake or other seismic activity.

Perhaps there was a global pole shift to cause a disaster such as this.

If there is a pole shift, it would cause a shift in the Earth's axis. The land masses would stop moving while the air and water continue to spin. The result is a series of devastating disasters. In many places, the earth's molten sub-layer would break through, and spread a sea of white hot liquid fire. This sea of hot fire would cook many cities and blow them up like a nuclear bomb. A shift in the Earth's axis could cause a two-mile-high wall of water, mud, and debris to sweep across the country, burying cities like Los Angeles and San Francisco under miles of violent seas and mud. River dams could break, and rivers could change course. The earth would experience extreme temperature changes that freeze everything solid within four hours. There would be the destruction of major cities, the emergence of new polar areas, and the evolution of the surviving humans into a new stone age.

Maybe a pole shift occurred, and all the things above occurred to cause a mud flood reset event!

Perhaps the magnetic field of the Earth can be manipulated upon its grid points, and slight pole shifts can be precisely engineered to either create a flooding scenario, or fiery scenario. Maybe this is how resets are always done between astrological ages.

Sorting Through Disinformation in Tartaria Land

Here are some alternative theories that aim to moderate the exaggerated content that is often found in social media related to the Mud Flood reset.

Tartaria = Germania: Rather than using the term Tartaria, it may be more accurate to refer to the last civilization as "Germania" or the "French Empire", given that the last global empire was centered in Western Europe and not Tartaria. Many of the buildings that are often referred to as "Tartarian" are actually European in style and are not located in areas that were once called Tartaria on old maps.

Giants = Aryan Race: While it has been suggested that genetic re-engineering may have occurred between resets, the idea that humans were giants 200 years ago is often mixed with fantastical claims. Mud Flood theorists frequently suggest that the giants were eliminated through genetic engineering to make them shorter during the 1830s reset. Instead of this, it may be more plausible to consider that the Germanic tribe was genetically engineered into existence as a subset of Aryans during a reset, and/or Americans were genetically engineered into existence. While there may have been giants thousands of years ago, there is little evidence to support the notion that the so-called Tartarians were giants. Perhaps different sub-races of the Aryan race have been engineered between resets to produce various ethnic groups.

Flat Earth = Engineered Earth: It is possible that Earth was terraformed a long time ago so that the sun and moon appear to be the same size on Earth. It is possible that CGI images were faked as well as the moon landing. While there are peculiar anomalies with the mainstream narrative about our planet, it does not mean our Earth is flat. It is conceivable that we have a larger engineered Earth with hidden continents. Or that our earth is engineered so that it is possible to manipulate its magnetic field on grid points to engineer pole shifts and natural disasters.

Free Energy = Different Technology Before Reset: We never had free energy. Rent has never been free! Maybe we had different forms of energy. Instead of gas power, we had hydroelectric, steam technology, helium airships, radium fireplaces, quartz light bulbs, and free use of radium and mercury. If people had electricity, even if it was wireless electricity, it was hydroelectric generated. And they likely paid for it like we pay for Wi-Fi and internet service today.

It may be difficult for the Reset genre of information to be visible to normies who consider themselves logical and reasonable if it includes topics like Giants, Tartaria, "Free Energy", and "Flat Earth." Perhaps this is intentional! The masses tend to reject or disregard the truth if it is associated with concepts lacking credibility.

Do Ages Switch Between Air, Water, and Fire based Utilities?

Are utilities switched out between resets based on the Occult Elements of Water, Fire, Earth, and Air? Perhaps steampunk, hydroelectric, and other water-based tech was prevalent in the Tartarian age, but dismantled during the reset. And gas combustion, fire-based energy prevalent in today's Modern age will be switched out in the future. Maybe the only way to survive a reset is to live off the grid, or not be connected to public utility services when a reset occurs.

After the mud flood, steam tech may have been disabled, such as steam-powered water treatment plants and toilets. Forms of alchemical energy could have been phased out, like the widespread use of radium and mercury in fireplaces, lights, and lighthouses. The use of helium in airships could have become unavailable. Perhaps a few reset-people were allowed to operate their radium-based or wireless-based fireplaces until the radium eventually burnt off, or the wireless power station stopped generating electricity. Eventually, people were forced to live in a new stone age until gas-powered appliances were rolled out.

Likewise, in the future, gas and oil based energy might be switched out for light or air-based power. Perhaps solar and wind energy will be the only permitted means to generate electricity.

Today, leftists believe that gas and oil should be phased out gradually. Leftists believe gas is unsustainable, and people will run out of oil from the earth's natural resources. People are being told now that natural gas leads to climate change and greenhouse gas emissions. Countries or companies are investing in other energy technologies that are considered renewable, such as solar and wind. The UN and liberal places have placed informal agreements to phase this type of energy out. Conservatives believe leftist's futuristic ideas will lead us into a stone age.

Maybe conservatives are right that a stone age will occur once oil and gas use is phased out. This stone age could kick off with an engineered, catastrophic reset. Thereafter, the military could forcibly disable or destroy any appliances or vehicles which once used gas, and disconnect any major utilities, such as water, sanitation, and gas utilities. Perhaps we will all suffer a reset like the mud flood, and people will have to do without their modern tech. Maybe people in a future age will believe that we lived without toilets, dishwashers, washing machines, cars, iphones, AI, or any means to generate electricity for all with gas and electric companies. We pooped in buckets and didn't wash our hands afterwards!

If some of today's modern humans are lucky enough to survive reset, they may have to participate in the conspiracy that denies any of this gas-based tech existed! Perhaps they will only be able to operate their dishwashers, toilets, and washing machines on their own personal solar power until these appliances inevitably fall into disrepair.

Ancient Windmills

Is there evidence that wind was a source of energy in the past! Of course! To this day, there are a few surviving vertical axis-windmills in Persia.

154

The Nashtifan Windmills are a series of ancient windmills located in the town of Nashtifan in Khorasan Province, Iran. These windmills are believed to be the oldest and largest windmills in the world, dating back to the 7th century AD. They have been designated as a UNESCO World Heritage Site in recognition of their cultural and historical significance.

The windmills were originally designed and constructed to harness the strong winds that blow through the surrounding hills and to grind grain into flour. They consist of a series of wooden blades that are mounted on a vertical axis and rotate when the wind blows. The rotational motion of the blades is then transferred through a series of gears to a large grinding stone, which grinds the grain into flour.

The Nashtifan Windmills are unique in that they are entirely made of wood, including the blades, the gears, and the base. They are also notable for their size, with some of the windmills standing up to 15 meters tall. Despite their age and their traditional design, the windmills are still in use today and continue to be an important source of flour for the local community.

According to a National Geographic Youtube video posted January 22, 2017, Mr. Latta Body is the last remaining caretaker of the windmills and has devoted his life to their protection. Unfortunately, there has been little interest in taking up the job from him.

D.U.M.B.S.

Deep Underground Military Bases

Did humanity survive catastrophes by taking refuge within tunnels underground? Do D.U.M.B.S. have something to do with these ancient tunnels?

"D.U.M.B.S." stands for "Deep Underground Military Bases." These are alleged secret underground facilities that are said to be operated by the United States military and other government agencies.

According to theory, these underground bases are located in remote areas and are used for a variety of purposes, such as storing weapons and equipment, conducting experiments, and providing a safe haven for government officials in case of a disaster or attack.

Some conspiracy theorists claim that these underground bases are part of a larger conspiracy to create a "New World Order" or to conduct secret experiments on the population. Others suggest that they are part of a larger network of tunnels and facilities that stretch across the United States and beyond. Perhaps those involved with the New World Order know who must be saved to ensure the continued existence of humanity, and are working to guide us towards a new era.

155

FEMA and Martial Law

The Deep State's plans for the next reset?

The Federal Emergency Management Agency (FEMA) is a government agency in the United States responsible for coordinating the response to disasters and emergencies that occur in the country. While FEMA does not have the power to declare martial law, some theories suggest that the agency is part of a larger plan to impose martial law in the United States.

Martial law is the imposition of military rule on a civilian population, often in response to a crisis or emergency situation. It involves the suspension of certain civil liberties and the transfer of power from civilian authorities to military commanders.

Some people believe that FEMA is secretly preparing for the imposition of martial law in the United States in response to a future crisis or disaster. They point to the agency's stockpiling of emergency supplies, the construction of detention centers, and other actions as evidence of a sinister plan to impose martial law.

FEMA allegedly has an interim government that mimics the structure of the U.S.'s current government. In their system, inferiors must refer to those above them as "Mr. President" or "Mr. Vice President". This entire interim government is to take over if a disaster such as a reset occurs. FEMA has plans for who will be saved, and who will not.

COVID conspiracy theorists fear FEMA camps because they believe that the government is planning to use them as a way to round up and imprison those who refuse to comply with COVID-related mandates, such as vaccination or quarantine orders. FEMA has the authority to quarantine individuals if they are deemed to be a threat to public health. This power is granted by the Public Health Service Act and has been used in the past to quarantine individuals during outbreaks of infectious diseases.

Alex Jones has discussed the theory of FEMA camps and guillotines on his show and website Infowars. He has made claims that the government is stockpiling guillotines and building FEMA camps as part of a plot to create a totalitarian New World Order. According to these conspiracy theorist sensationalists, perhaps those executed by guillotines could be used as organ donors or the source of intact and viable cells for cloning purposes!

156

Do Urban Explorers Know Something we don't?

Are they discovering old Tunnels that people used to escape the mud flood?

An Abandoned Mansion [157]

Some urban explorers love wandering around old abandoned sites, like the Proper People on Youtube. The Proper People explore abandoned or hidden urban spaces, such as abandoned prisons, mental hospitals, religious schools, gilded mansions, amusement parks. They almost always find tunnels underneath these structures. These buildings are often inaccessible to the public or seem dangerous and shady. If you watch their videos, you'll notice that these places always seem conveniently open to them. They always warn the public that they could fall into a hole or have something fall on them if they explore the same places, as the premises are not designed to be safe. There also lies a risk of being arrested for trespass.

Some of their videos show places that are downright creepy. They will show mental hospitals designed for children with wheelchairs, electroshock machines, surgery tables, and overhead lamps. Old mansions will be lined with graffiti, mold, and broken glass.

Maybe these guys know something we don't and are telling us something. Were some of these spaces used as Safe Spaces from the Mud Flood? Were some of these places used to raise orphans after the Reset? Do some of the places show ancient technology that people possessed before the mud flood? Could some of these places be used to survive the next reset?

In any case, one can learn that there are many old abandoned sites that have tunnels. Including old prisons, mines, train stations, old religious schools, theme parks, military buildings, mental hospitals, and factories.

If Our Ancestors Were Clones, Who Were the Originals?

The meaning of "Born Again"?

Many mud flood theorists believe the earth was repopulated with clones or people spawned in cabbage patch-like machines in the 1880s.

If we are to entertain this insane theory, how would it go? Could martial law be consistently implemented during end-time disasters, resulting in the systematic killing of individuals seeking refuge underground, followed by their cloning for rebirth? These clones could then be raised in institutions located in the same place as the original people who disappeared underground. For example, those who sought refuge in a mine shaft could be found and cloned, only to be reborn and raised as coal miners. Similarly, those who fled into a railroad tunnel could become cloned orphans riding the orphan train, while those who took refuge in prisons could become citizens of a penal colony such as Australia or Georgia. Those hiding beneath factories might be killed, and their clones used as child laborers in workhouses. Mental patients could be reborn in mental hospitals. Those who took refuge under a church could have a clone raised in a Catholic Board School.

Or perhaps we should go with an allegory along Christian lines. Those who are given a proper Christian religious burial could somehow be raised from the dead, their bodies cloned, and their DNA given new life through some super high tech birthing machine for a new civilization. This could give all new meaning to the phrase "born again". This book is simply documenting crazy theories. It is not meant to offend anyone.

The Biggest Secret in Freemasonry: The Mud Flood

What if freemasonry's biggest secret is the Mud Flood? What if all of history is a lie, and humanity experiences cycles of growth, peak, decay, catastrophe, and reset in which old technology and knowledge is lost? What if our resets and apocalypses actually happen every 200 years rather than every 10,000 years, and that we experienced a reset as recent as 1830? What if humanity experienced a flood in which the whole earth was covered in a layer of mud and humanity experienced massive depopulation? Perhaps this is the secret that is revealed once a freemason achieves one of their highest degrees.

Most of Freemasonry's teachings are based on allegories involving pre-Mud Flood neoclassical architectural features that were commonly used before 1830. Freemasonry is a "peculiar system of morality, veiled in allegory and illustrated by symbols.". When one is initiated into freemasonry, he may find the ritual like a strange play. This scripted drama involves architects building the ancient Temple of King Solomon. The beginning of the play has a male enter a temple guarded by an outer and inner guard, with a long procedure in which the lodge is "closed tyled" or walled off from the outside. The teachings within the ritual involve moral lessons from architectural tools that we don't use anymore. A freemason is taught lessons to act upright as shown by the plumb rule, act on the level using the level tool, act within defining limits shown by a compass, or square their actions using the square. Freemasons are taught to develop wisdom, strength, and beauty as represented by the Ionic, Doric and Corinthian columns. But since these types of columns aren't used in architecture anymore, freemasons must learn what these columns looked like. A freemason may acquire the Royal Arch degree of freemasonry and wear a pin that represents a Keystone in an Arch, yet we don't build with Arches with keystones like in the old days. Their passwords are often based on architectural features in a mythical temple, like Boaz and Jachin representing two pillars in that temple. Their outfits feature aprons alluding to outfits worn by cathedral architects.

We don't build cathedrals anymore. Yet freemasons claim their system originated from the builders of the cathedrals, and wear aprons like these original architects. We don't build stone castles anymore. But the freemasons claim their system originated from Knights who dwelled within castles. Their entire system is supposed to 'polish the rough ashlar', or polish off your character in preparation for building. But we don't build pyramids. Or giant stone architecture with special interlocking stones like the Incans. Yet freemasons still have rituals wherein they lay large cornerstones of buildings. Their temples often look like some ancient Egyptian pyramid.

So perhaps the big masonic reveal is: We don't build with old-style arches, obelisks, columns, or enormous stone and brick wondrous buildings for a reason: Because we suffered a mud flood! And these buildings with these architectural features hold that secret within plain sight! Look how all these buildings with these features are half buried!

But what is the freemason's system of morality? Do they have a list of right and wrong like a Christian Church? Likely not. Their morality depends on what time it is. How far away from the last reset we are.   It's a planetary system. Just like the planets rule each day in the week, a planet may rule a particular span of time between resets. Each generation within a reset is guided to act in a certain way depending on whether they're the first, second, third, fourth generation after the Reset. The Great generation was led through a war. Boomers were led through peak economic times. Generation X conservatives were indoctrinated in libertarianism for open borders or for liberalism to limit urban sprawl and build dense city centers. Millennials and Zoomers are also molded to have a different character and experience different worldwide events. Just like the days of the week, each generation is ruled by a planet and a character governing their time. Freemasons indoctrinate each group with a belief system that will support a particular series of events and agenda. Freemasons love to polarize people and have a dichotomy between Right and Left just like their pillars Jachin and Boaz. As soon as you think you've figured out the political system, they switch up the entire dialogue for the next generation. Yes, "they" switch it up. The guys behind closed doors, coordinating as a group in secret away from us, within their close tyled lodge.

Do Resets Look Similar To The Rapture From the Left Behind Series?

Will the Reset Look Similar to the rapture as described by the Left Behind book series? In the Left Behind book series from the 90s, a rapture event occurred, in which believers in Christ were taken up to heaven. According to the books, the Rapture occurs suddenly, and true believers in Christ, regardless of denomination, are taken up to heaven in an instant. Their bodies are transformed, and they are taken up to be with God while their clothes and possessions are left behind. Those who are not believers in Christ are left behind to face a time of tribulation on earth, which is the main focus of the series.

158

Has an event similar to the Rapture occurred in the past, where people were taken along with their clothes and personal belongings, leaving only the architectural structures?

Pictured below is part of a panorama of Paris from the 1800s. What you will see is a total lack of people and anything not permanently attached. Horses, carts, litter, fruit stands, porch furniture, potted plants, etc. Some say the only possible explanation is a gravitational event that swept the land clean. Was everything somehow sucked into space!

Project BlueBeam

159

  Many conspiracy theorists believe in a military plan called Project BlueBeam. This is a conspiracy theory that claims that the United States government, or possibly a shadowy group of powerful individuals, is planning to use advanced technology to create a false flag alien invasion or a false flag second coming of Jesus Christ in order to gain control over the population. The theory suggests that the project would involve a staged event, which could include the use of holographic images, space-based lasers, or other advanced technologies, to create a convincing illusion of an extraterrestrial or divine event.

  The conspiracy theory has been circulating online since the 1990s and is often tied to other theories such as the New World Order or the Illuminati. Proponents of the theory argue that the ultimate goal of Project Blue Beam is to create a one-world government or a new world religion that will be controlled by the conspirators.

  Well, perhaps there already is a one-world government, and it will engineer a Reset that looks like a series of natural disasters, war, or famine. Maybe it plans to stage a rapture-like event to kick off the next astrological age.

Why so many Zombie Apocalypse Movies?

Conspiracy theorists believe that the Illuminati must warn you of their plans. This is known as "predictive programming." This theory suggests that the Illuminati or other secretive organizations use various forms of media, such as movies, TV shows, music videos, and video games, to communicate their plans to the general public in advance. The idea is that by exposing the public to these plans through popular culture, the Illuminati can manipulate and control the masses into accepting their agenda without resistance. Those who believe in this theory often point to supposed examples of predictive programming in popular media, such as references to the 9/11 attacks in movies and TV shows that aired before the event. An alternative idea is that when a movie is watched by a large number of people, it increases the likelihood of a comparable event occurring by influencing the mystical realm.

160

Was predictive programming the reason why there were so many zombie apocalypse movies from 2010 and beyond? Do these movies resemble our controller's plans? Some popular zombie pandemic movies include:

1. Resident Evil: Afterlife (2010) - Alice fights against the Umbrella Corporation and its zombies to save the survivors of a Los Angeles prison outbreak.
2. The Walking Dead (2010-2022 TV Series) - Set in a world overrun by zombies, a group of survivors must navigate their way through danger and uncertainty.
3. World War Z (2013) - A former United Nations investigator is tasked with finding the source of a global zombie pandemic and stopping it before it's too late.
4. Train to Busan (2016) - A father and daughter try to survive a zombie outbreak on a train to Busan, South Korea.
5. The Girl with All the Gifts (2016) - A scientist and a teacher protect a young girl who may be the key to saving humanity from a zombie outbreak.
6. Cargo (2017) - A man in Australia tries to find a safe haven for his infant daughter during a zombie outbreak.

7. Day of the Dead: Bloodline (2018) - A group of military personnel and survivors try to survive a zombie outbreak in an underground bunker.
8. Overlord (2018) - American paratroopers encounter supernatural forces behind enemy lines on the eve of D-Day.
9. Kingdom (2019- TV Series) - A prince investigates a mysterious plague that turns people into zombies in medieval Korea.
10. Black Summer (2019- TV Series) - Set in the same universe as Z Nation, a group of survivors try to escape a zombie-infested city during the early days of the outbreak.
11. Blindness (2008) - A mysterious epidemic causes people to lose their sight, and a group of blind people are forced to survive in a quarantined city.
12. Bird Box (2018) - A woman and her two children must navigate a world filled with supernatural entities that cause people to see their worst fears and commit suicide.
13. The Silence (2019) - A family must navigate a world overrun by creatures that hunt by sound, forcing them to live in silence.
14. Perfect Sense (2011) - A chef and a scientist fall in love as a global epidemic causes people to lose their senses, one at a time.
15. Blind Mountain (2007) - A young woman is sold into marriage and taken to a remote mountain village where she is held captive and forced to marry a man who is blind.
16. 28 Days Later (2002) - After a virus wipes out most of humanity, a small group of survivors must fight to stay alive in a world overrun by zombies.
17. Zombieland (2009) - A group of survivors navigate their way through a post-apocalyptic world filled with zombies and other dangers.

After the filming of all these zombie pandemic movies, the Covid pandemic rolled around in 2020. Perhaps everyone accepted the sudden takeover of power by authority due to these movies.

Why are there so many Post-Apocalyptic Movies?

Similarly, there are a lot of movies and TV shows about a post-apocalyptic world after a major depopulation event. These include:

- The Walking Dead (TV Series): 2010 - ongoing, set in a world overrun by zombies, a group of survivors must navigate their way through danger and uncertainty.
- 28 Days Later (Movie): 2002, a man wakes up from a coma to find that a virus has wiped out most of humanity, and he must fight to survive in a world of infected, zombie-like creatures.
- The Road (Movie): 2009, a father and son journey across a post-apocalyptic wasteland, facing danger and despair as they try to survive.
- The Book of Eli (Movie): 2010, a lone warrior travels across a post-apocalyptic America, protecting a valuable book that may hold the key to saving humanity.
- I Am Legend (Movie): 2007, a lone survivor in New York City must fend off infected, vampire-like creatures and find a cure for the virus that has decimated humanity.
- The Last Man on Earth (TV Series): 2015-2018, a man who thinks he is the last human on Earth must learn to survive and cope with his isolation.
- The Leftovers (TV Series): 2014-2017, after 2% of the world's population mysteriously disappears, those left behind struggle to make sense of what has happened and find a way to move forward.
- Snowpiercer (Movie and TV Series): 2013 (movie) / 2020 - ongoing (TV series), a train carrying the last remnants of humanity travels through a frozen wasteland, but class divisions and power struggles threaten to destroy the fragile society onboard.
- Revolution (TV Series): 2012-2014, after a global blackout, society has collapsed and people must adapt to a world without electricity and technology.
- The Colony (TV Series): 2009-2010, a group of survivors in a post-apocalyptic world must band together to fend off threats and rebuild their community.

Do these apocalyptic movies show plans of a future reset? Are these examples of predictive programming, or are they just entertaining movies?

The Next Reset: Where and When?

Often the elite disclose their plans behind closed doors. But publish documents to let you know their plans publicly.

Where

Could disaster strike areas in the world that will be part of future megaregions?

States have formed multi state compacts, and planned megaregions for different purposes like fighting Covid. They published maps of future megaregions for the United States. 5G Smart Megaregions would be ultra-dense and form high tech cities.

Environmentalists have mapped out specific environmental and biodiversity zones. They have circled areas in which humans should not occupy to protect diverse plant and animal species.

When

When could a reset occur? Some theorize that the next reset will be in 2030 based on global treaties. Agenda 21 is a sustainable development treaty agreed upon by many countries. Many people believe that the Covid pandemic of 2021 was related to Agenda 21, as it rolled out many of its plans under the guise of fighting Covid. Covid was touted as a Global Reset. Agenda 30 is the next important world treaty to promote sustainable development. Perhaps another big happening like Covid will occur in 2030 to impact human behavior and population.

Others theorize that a large reset could occur in 2040.   They follow the website Archaix which predicts natural disasters every 138 years. Jason Breshears' website, Archaix claims a solar minimum will occur in the year 2040, and could be the time of a large reset. He also claims that funny things happen in our simulation like red rain or celestial events.

Still others claim that 2045 could be a reset. 2045 is an interesting year because the United States may reach its cover target race-ratio of ½ White, ¼ Latin American, ⅛ African American, 1/16 Asian American, 1/16 other.

Is 2050 a reset date? Many countries plan to be carbon neutral by 2050. Perhaps the elites use the word "carbon" as a code for human life, as carbon is the main element in organic compounds that make up human bodies Several countries and groups have set carbon neutrality goals for 2050, such as the United States, Japan, China, the United Kingdom, Canada, Australia, and the European Union."

How

How would a reset go down? Disaster analysts claim that famine in our society could be imminent. Supply chains could collapse. Food factories seem to have been destroyed from mysterious events. Perhaps a climate disaster like cold weather could cause a collapse in the food supply chain.

Pandemics often follow famine. There were so many Zombie Pandemic movies made around the 2010's that perhaps a viral pandemic will cause a massive depopulation event. Most pandemic movies start with viral zombies initially, and eventually devolve into a shootout. Those with great sharpshooter skills often pick up food at an empty convenience store.

If the last reset involved flooding, perhaps the next reset involves fire. Perhaps under the guise of nuclear attack. Famines and pandemics often trigger wars. Citizens revolt once their government proves incompetent to handle disasters.

How would one survive a Reset?

Does anyone survive a reset according to Mud Flood theorists, or is it a complete wipeout? Do Covenant members like Freemasons or Satanist have a higher likelihood of survival? Does one need to be whisked away into underground tunnels via their secret deep state or societal connection? If they are whisked away, are they cloned, or do they survive in the same body?

Perhaps 21st Century Safe Spaces will resemble 19th Century Sites with Tunnels. Potential Spots with Underground Tunnels with 30 years of FEMA supplies could be:
- FEMA Camps underneath Walmarts
- Mine Shafts
- Gas, Electric, Fiber Optic Utilities
- Tesla's SpaceX tunnels which will zip Cars through tunnels
- Train Stations
- Military Bases
- Select Churches, Universities, and Schools with Secret Tunnels
- Factories

Perhaps individuals can create their own safe space from disaster. Surviving a disaster may require a suitable shelter underground and maybe 30 years of food and water.

However, is it really best to survive it? Or to become "born again" through a ritual cloning and DNA software update process? Would you rather your heirs be a future indigenous people hanging on to past DNA chains, or the updated version of humans with the latest greatest DNA hooked into bluetooth suffering from cultural amnesia?

Who Will be Selected to Survive Reset?

The people most likely to survive a reset is anyone's guess.

Maybe Project Bluebeam, martial law, and a money reset are all planned for our future. If there is a reset, those who survive it will need to comply with the military to rewrite history. If freedoms have to be given, and monitoring is required, those who survive will comply.

Maybe the 'Illuminati' help select those who are resilient who have a strong instinct to survive. If so, maybe they would tell those with a tough independent mindset how to prep. Are they schooling those who want to hang onto old Aryan chains of DNA in surviving reset?

If the Illuminati really are in charge, would they want those who survive to to be vaccinated or unvaccinated? If the goal is to change DNA, maybe the vaccine provides a necessary DNA update. On the other hand, perhaps the illuminati consider anyone who takes the vaccine as too stupid and docile for the next age.

Are those who's beliefs line up with the future more likely to be selected? Maybe those in the top secret societies have already proven that their beliefs line up with the New World Order and are more likely to survive.

Endnotes

1. The Cathedral Church of Saint John the Divine, by Simon Absonditus, licensed under CC by 3.0
2. All Gizah Pyramids, Ricardo Liberato, licensed under CC by 2.0
3. The stone wall of Nijo-jo japan, Tomomarusan, licensed under CC by 4.0
4. Sacsayhuaman in Cuzco, Peru, photo by Jorge Manriquez P., licensed under CC by 3.0.jpg
5. The Lion Gate at Mycenae, Greece, 1250 BC, JoyofMuseums, licensed under CC by 4.0
6. Ancient Kassope walls Greece, Harry Gouvas, licensed under CC
7. Adalaj stepwell from above carved in sandstone, Karthik Easvur, licensed under CC by 4.0
8. Sun temple Surya kund Stepwell adjoining the temple, Kinjalps, licensed under CC by 3.0
9. Rani ki vav, by Bernard Gagnon, licensed under CC by 3.0
10. Chand Baori Stepwell, photo by Gerd Eichmann, licensed under CC by 2.0
11. Le temple de Brihadishwara (Tanjore, India), by Jean-Pierre Dalbera, licensed under CC by 2.0
12. Lakshmi Narasimha temple, by Dineshkannambadi, licensed under CC by 3.0.jpg
13. Kailash Temple, Ellora by Kunal Mukherjee, licensed under CC by 2.0
14. Fuerte de Nuestra Señora de Gracia, Elvas, Portugal
15. Fort Bourtange, Dack9, licensed under CC by 4.0
16. Fort Manjarabad, Karnataka, India, Jakeer Hussain Visuals, licensed under CC by 4.0
17. Duomo di Milano in Milan, photo by Jakub Halun, licensed under CC by 4.0
18. Notre Dame in Paris, by Peter Haaz, licensed under CC by 3.0.jpg
19. Wells Cathedral Nave, Michael D Beckwith, licensed under CC by 1.0
20. Prang Pyramid, Cambodia, public domain
21. Chichen Itza, Mexico, photo by Daniel Schwen, licensed under CC by 4.0
22. Kheops Pyramid, Egypt, photo by Nina, licensed under CC by 2.5
23. Bosnian Sun Pyramid Lookout, photo by TheBIHLover, licensed under CC by 4.0
24. Sphinx at Universitetskaya Embankment in Saint Petersburg, photo by Florstein, licensed under CC by 4.0
25. Bucegi Sphinx - Romania, photo by Radu Privantu, licensed under CC by 2.0
26. Valley of Ghosts, Crimea, photo by Vovenarg, licensed under CC by 3.0
27. The Sphinx, Ischigualasto, Argentina, photo by user idobi, licensed under CC by 3.0
28. Pakistan Natural Sphinx, Balochistan, photo by Bilal Mirza, licensed under CC by 2.0
29. Great Sphinx of Giza, photo by MusikAnimal, licensed under CC by 3.0
30. Hephaistos temple, Athens, Greece, photo by Tommi Nikkila, licensed under CC by 3.0
31. Tempio Canoviano-Possagno, Italy, photo by mrlov, licensed under CC by 2.0
32. Crimean War 1854, Church of St Peter and St Paul, located near St. Petersburg, Russia, public domain
33. Baalbek Baccustempel, Lebanon, photo by Jan Hilgers, licensed under CC by 3.0

34. Walhalla wie Parthenon, Germany, photo by Wolfgang Pehlemann, licensed under CC by 3.0

35. The Parthenon in Nashville, Tennessee, photo by White Alister, T., licensed under CC by 4.0

36. Siegestor in Munich, photo by Martin Falbisoner, licensed under CC by 3.0

37. Zafar Arch, Afghanistan, photo by Kowsari, licensed under CC by 4.0

38. Leptis Magna Arch of Septimus Severus, Libya, public domain

39. The Soldiers and Sailors Arch, Brooklyn, NY, photo by WT shared Padraic, licensed under CC by 4.0

40. Washington Square Park in New York City., photo by Self, licensed under CC by 3.0

41. Hyde Park Obelisk, Sydney, photo by Kgbo, licensed under CC by 4.0

42. Obelisk of Thutmose III, in Istanbol, public domain

43. The Rome Stele in Ethiopia, photo by Ondrej Zvacek, licensed under CC by 1.2

44. Obelisk in Munich, photo by Martin Dosch, licensed under CC by 3.0

45. Roma Obelisco Laterano, photo by Manousek, licensed under CC by 2.0

46. The Caesarea Maritima obelisk at dusk, Israel, photo by Oren Rozen, licensed under CC by 4.0

47. https://www.vintag.es/2013/03/panorama-photos-of-san-francisco-1878.html

48. Duppa-Montgomery Adobe House, by Tony the Marine, licensed under CC by 3.0

49. Side view of the Casa Grande Ruins, photo by Tony the Marine (talk) licensed under CC by 3.0

50. https://en.wikipedia.org/wiki/Salt_Lake_Tabernacle

51. https://en.wikipedia.org/wiki/Salt_Lake_Tabernacle

52. Iowa State Capitol, by Danksergeant15, licensed by CC at 4.0

53.   St. Mary's Magdalene Church dropped over 20 feet in elevation during the Dodge Street Regrading Project in Omaha, Nebraska. The door that was used is 20 feet high. The official narrative is that the bottom floor was built after the road was regraded due a process called underpinning. Mud flood theorists don't buy it! They believe the first floor was buried, and had to be dug out

54. Seattle Underground, photo by Rennett Stowe, licensed under CC by 2.0

55. US Census Population Graph from 1790, by Crotalus Horridus, licensed under CC by 3.0

56. California fire in 2017 in Santa Rosa, photo by California National Guard, Public Domain, licensed under CC by 2.0

57. Engraving depicting Sherman's march to the sea. Original from 1868 by L. Stebbins

58. Building made of Staff at Amusement Park at Coney Island

59. https://chicagology.com/columbiaexpo/fair033/

60. Westinghouse: The Life and Times of an American Icon.   Documentary.

61. Encyclopedia of Chicago, http://www.encyclopedia.chicagohistory.org/pages/1386.html

62. Rosenberg, C. M. (2008). Fin De Siecle and Beyond. America at the fair: Chicago's 1893 World's Columbian Exposition (pp. 260-279). Charleston, SC: Arcadia Pub..

63. Larson, Erik (2003). *The Devil in the White City: Murder, Magic, and Madness at the Fair That Changed America*. New York: Vintage Books. pp. 318–320.

64. Looted head of a lamassu, photo by Osama Shukir Muhammed Amin FRCP(Glasg), licensed under CC by 4.0

65. Temple of Bel, photo by Bernard Gagnan, licensed under CC by 3.0

66. Ionosphere_and_its_constituents by Space Travel Blog Rute Marta Jansone, licensed under CC by 4.0

67. Steamy Manhole in New York City, by Diego Torres Silvestre, licensed under CC by 2.0

68. Saint Wellington Arch, by Jim Osley, licensed under CC by 2.0. And horseshoe magnet by Oguraclutch, licensed by CC under 3.0

69. Dome of Saint-Peter's Basilica., by Jakub T. Jankiewicz, licensed under CC by 3.0. Antennae, by F5oux, licensed under CC by 4.0

70. spire, by fots2, licensed under CC by 3.0.jpg

71. Resonant Cavity Magnetron, by Vanessa Ezekowitz, licensed under CC by 3.0

72. Wells Cathedral Saxon baptismal font, by Gene Hawkins, Licensed under CC by 2.0

73. Model of a Soviet Tokamak, photograph by Sergey Rodovnichenko, licensed under CC by 2.0

74. Obelisk in Acton Park, by Allen Murray-Rust, LIcensed under CC by 2.0

75. Researchers Turn Stone Into a Battery for Your Future Smart Home Systems, Hackster. by Gareth Halfacree, July 2022

76. Dome at Verona, by BEIC, licensed under CC by 4.0

77. Ruins of Column in Puerta Oscura, by Daniel Capilla, licensed under CC by 4.0.jpg

78. The Temple of Apollo at Corinth, by Berthold Werner, licensed under CC by 3.0

79. Red Brick Schoolhouse, Wiscasset, ME, by Kenneth Zirkel, licensed under CC by 3.0

80. Network World, Disruptor, by Patrick Nelson, October 12, 2020.

81. St. Pancras Railway Station, by Mark Ahsmann, licensed under CC by 3.0

82. Satirical Print produced in 1781

83. A photograph of the Decatur Water Works I took on a hike through Georgia

84. Fort Bourtange, Dack9, licensed under CC by 4.0

85. Shukhov Tower, photo by Maxim Fedorov, licensed under CC by 3.0

86. Combined Sewer Overflow Diagram, Source US EPA

87. Derinkuyu Underground City in Cappadocia, Turkey, photo by Nevit Dilmen, Licensed under CC by 3.0.

88. Gaddis, V. H. (1991). Tunnels of the Titans. In Native American Myths & Mysteries (pp. 79-92). Barnes & Noble Books

89. https://pba.pbslearningmedia.org/resource/hopi-origin-story/hopi-origin-story/

90. https://pba.pbslearningmedia.org/resource/hopi-origin-story/hopi-origin-story/

91. Disinganno, Cappella Sansevero, by David Sivyer, licensed under CC by 2.0

92. The Kidnapping of Proserpina, photo by Int3gr4te, licensed under Creative Commons by 3.0

93. Veiled Lady, Artist Corradini, photo by Didier Descouens, licensed under CC by 4.0

94. A puzzle ball on display at the Overseas Museum, Bremen, photo by Elfenbeinschnitzerei Breman Overseas Museum, licensed under CC by 4.0

95. Civil War Graveyard, Photograph of Alexandria National Cemetery, Virginia with wooden markers, 1862-69

96. Prague's Old Astronomical Clock, photo by Steve Collis, licensed under CC by 2.0

97. The sun's trajectory on the sky on different solstices and equinoxes, drawing by Slancestoene.png, licensed under GNU General Public License

98. Dubois, Jean (1987), The Fundamentals of Esoteric Knowledge.

99 My own image, I drew with Google Sheets, Paint, and public domain astrological symbols

100 Generation timeline, by Cmglee, licensed under CC by 4.0

101 Picture of Woodstock, photo by James M Shelley, licensed under CC by 4.0

102 LGBT, photo by AndrewRM, licensed under CC by 3.0

103 Races of Egypt (from left to right):An Egyptian, an Asiatic, a Libyan, and a Nubian. This drawing is by an unknown artist copying murals of the tomb of Seti I;

104 Google Earth. (2023). [Satellite image of the North Pole]. Retrieved March 8, 2023. From https://earth.google.com/web/search/north+pole/@85,-135,83.32268805a,0.00989313d,35y,0h,45t,0r/data=CnUaSxJFCiUweDRmOTMONGRhOTUxNWI5NTE6MHgONTE4ZDBjNGQ1YzY4ODc2GTWglP_f1ZAIQAAAAAA4GDAKgpub3JOaCBwb2xlGAIgASImCiQJmaT4zr78UkARWJzKhoK8UEAZeJCwXxOBWOAhk5FRBrn2YsAoAg

105. Door from San Giovanni in Laterano, Darafsh, licensed under CC by 3.0

106. Entrance to The Pantheon, Rome, Italy, Ank Kumar, licensed under CC by 4.0

107. The Sons of God Saw the Daughters of Men That They Were Fair, by Daniel Chester French, modeled by 1918, carved 1923 - Corcoran Gallery of Art, public domain.jpg

108. The garderobe at Peveril Castle, Derbyshire, England

109. Quantitative analysis of population-scale family trees with millions of relatives, Science p. 171.

110. Bandelier National Monument, New Mexico Sarah Stierch, licensed under CC by 2.0

111. Bandelier National Monument, Cliff Dwellings, photo by Daniel Mayer, licensed under CC by 3.0

112. Facade of Ancient Church , photo by Klaus-Peter Simon, licensed under CC by 3.0

113.Rocce rosse (Red rocks) in Arbatax Sardinia, photo by Isiwal, licensed under CC by 4.0

114. The Palace Tomb, Petra, photo by Bernard Gagnon, licensed under CC by 3.0

115. Ruined castle in Ogrodzieniec, Kamil Porembiński, licensed under CC by 2.0

116. The Western Deffoeffa of Kerma, photo by Jac Strijbos8, licensed under CC by 3.0

117. House in Kandovan, Iran, photo by Dr. Nasser Haghighat, licensed under CC by 2.0

118. Setenil de las Bodegas, Andalucía (España), photo by El Pantera, licensed under CC by 4.0

119. Pompeii Excavations, Flickr Commons

120. Magnificent CME Erupts on the Sun, by NASA Goddard Space Flight Center, licensed under CC by 2.0

121. The stone wall of Nijo-jo japan wiki commons, photo by Tomomarusan, licensed under CC by 3.0

122. Veiled Lady, Artist Corradini, photo by Didier Descouens, licensed under CC by 4.0

123. Ancestral Shoshone Indian petroglyphs, 1000 to 2000 years old, White Mountain Petroglyphs, southwestern Wyoming, USA, photo by James St. John, licensed under CC by 2.0

124. Fort Bourtange, photo by Dack9, licensed under CC by 4.0

125. Cinta Muraria di Palmanova, photo by llirikllirik, licensed under CC by 1.0

126. (Top Left) Ceuta, Sleeping Lady Mountain Palace Colorado Mesa Verde, by Tobi 87, licensed under CC by 4.0

127. American Castle Panoramic Ha Ha Tonka State Park Missouri, by The PhotoRun, Jason Runyon, licensed under CC by 3.0.jpg

128. Coral Castle, Homestead, Florida, by Library of Congress, Public Domain.jpg

129. One of the largest genetic studies of South Americans to date is the Latin American Human Genome Project (LHG), which analyzed genetic data from over 6,000 individuals from five countries: Brazil, Chile, Colombia, Mexico, and Peru. The LHG study found that the average ancestry proportions in these countries are as follows:

- Brazil: 62% European, 21% Indigenous, and 17% African

- Chile: 44% European, 51% Indigenous, and 5% African

- Colombia: 49% European, 38% Indigenous, and 14% African

- Mexico: 41% Indigenous, 30% European, and 28% African

- Peru: 47% Indigenous, 37% European, and 16% African

130. Stoeckle, M. Y., & Thaler, D. S. (2018). Why should mitochondria define species? Human Evolution. Retrieved from https://www.biorxiv.org/content/10.1101/276717v2

131. Did 90% of Animal Species Appear about the Same Time as Human Beings?, by Joel Duff. Published in Biologos. July 24, 2018

132. Noah's Ark, oil on cavan painting by Edward Hicks, 1846 Philadelphia Museum of Art, public domain

133. Devils tower, photo by U.S. Geological Survey, Reston, VA, USA, licensed under CC by 2.0.jpg

134. Public domain.

135 (Top Left) Ceuta, Sleeping Lady Mountain, photo by Manuel Hdez Lafuente, licensed under CC by 3.0

136 (Top Right) The Grey Man of the Merrick, Scotland, photo by Scothill, licensed under CC by 3.0

137 (Middle Left) The Great Stone Face Rock, Pennington Gap, VA, photo by WarrDaddy, licensed under CC by 4.0

138 (Middle Right) Peña de los Enamorados Antequera, Malaga photo by Grez, licensed under CC by 2.0

139 (Bottom Left) Old Man of the park. Near Sundance, Wyo, public domain

140 (Bottom Right) Old Man of the Mountain, New Hampshire Wiki Commons

141. Elephant Rock in Iceland, photo by Diego Delso, licensed under CC by 4.0

142. Hvitserkur, Iceland, public domain

143. The Battle of Marduk and Tiamat from Pace of Sennacherib, Nimroud, Nineveh, photo by TYalaA, licensed under CC by 4.0

144. Flat Earth model, photo by Flatearthgifts, licensed under CC by 4.0

145. Flat earth, wiki commons, public domain

146. Nelson Mandela, photo by Kingkongphoto & www.celebrity-photos.com from Laurel, licensed under CC by 2.0

147. Cyclopedia universal history - 1895, Flickers the Commons

148. Crucifixion fresco from Visoki Dečani Monastery, public domain

149. Planets, public domain

150. 2018 Nibiru Planet X Breaking! Visible Planets in the Sky! Gif by Rogelioanguizola, licensed under CC by 4.0

151. Huxley - Mans Place in Nature, public domain

152. Australopithecus afarensis skull, photo by Tiia Monto, licensed under CC by 3.0

153. Amazing natural disasters, by no, licensed under CC by 4.0

154. Old Vertical Windmills in Nashtifan, Turkey, photo by Ali Vaseghnia, licensed under CC by 4.0.jpg

155. SAC command center, underground structure, Offutt Air Force Base, Strategic Air Command, Nebraska, public domain

156. FEMA Base Camp in Beaumont, public domain

157. An abandoned mansion, photo by Pavel Kirillov, licensed under CC by 2.0

158. An image generated with Shutterstock's AI

159. AI generated image from Shutterstock's AI
160. Zombie Apocalypse, photo by marsupium photography, licensed under CC by 2.0